GIL
MERRICK

KEITH DIXON

GIL MERRICK

breedon **books**
PUBLISHING

First published in Great Britain in 2009 by
The Breedon Books Publishing Company Limited
Breedon House, 3 The Parker Centre,
Derby, DE21 4SZ.

ISBN 978-1-85983-693-4

Printed and bound by TJ International Ltd, Padstow, Cornwall

——————— CONTENTS ———————

──────ACKNOWLEDGEMENTS──────

G rateful thanks to the following people and publications for their help with this book whether directly or indirectly: Julie, Holly, Matt, Ben and Harry Dixon, Gil and Ivy Merrick, Gordon Astall, Bertie Auld, Charles Buchan (publisher of *Charles Buchan's Football Monthly* and *Soccer Gift Book*), Ian Drew (publisher of *The Blues Magazine*), George Edwards, Winston Foster, Alex Govan, Colin Green, Jimmy Harris, Dean Hayes (author of *The St Andrew's Encyclopaedia*) Mike Hellawell, Andrew Henry (author of *Today's the Day*), Hyder Jawad (author of *Keep Right On*), Jack Lane, Tony Matthews (author of *Birmingham City –The Complete Record* and *Images of Sport – Birmingham City Football Club*), John Newman, Malcolm Page, Brian Sharples, Graham Sissons, Peter Waring (author of *Head to Head*), Trevor Wolstenholme and Michelle Harrison and the team at Breedon Books.

Images for this publication have been supplied by *Charles Buchan's Football Monthly*, *Charles Buchan's Soccer Gift Book*, *Blues Magazine*, *Birmingham Post and Mail* and private collections. Every effort has been made to identify the original source of other illustrations.

PREFACE

In 1954 at the age of 32 I published a book entitled *I See It All*. It is now 2009 and I am 87, celebrating the 70th anniversary of my signing professional terms for Birmingham City Football Club. Perhaps I should have entitled this book 'I've seen it all'!

In 1954 I had not appeared in an FA Cup Final at Wembley, I had not managed a First Division football club, I had not won a major trophy as a manager or appeared in European club football as a player and I had yet to experience the greatest disappointment of my football life! My Biography tells it all and a bit more!

But let's start with one of the regular questions I get asked today:

'What would be the best Blues side if you could pick players you played with?'

Gil Merrick, Ken Green, Billy Hughes, Fred Harris, Trevor Smith, Frank Mitchell, Jackie Stewart, Peter Murphy, Eddie Brown, Neil Dougall and George Edwards. Subs: Jeff Hall, Gordon Astall and Alex Govan.

I am extremely grateful to Ivan Barnsley, who brought me back from the wilderness. He visited me repeatedly while I was at Sports & Utilities asking me to rejoin the Bluenose fold through his Birmingham City Historical and Collectors' Society. For nearly three years I refused, but he never gave up and finally I gave in when he invited me to make an award to Malcolm Page. When I entered the room I was overwhelmed by the affection shown to me and decided then to re-engage with the fans.

My thanks also go to my author, Keith Dixon, who enticed me to participate in writing this book, a process that has evoked a whole host of memories, most of which are good. Finally to all you Bluenoses; it has been a great privilege to play in front of you for so many years through the good times (yes there were a few!) and the bad times. I will never forget you and the support you gave me throughout my career. Keep Right On!

Gil Merrick

──────INTRODUCTION──────

I t was the day before my eighth birthday, Christmas Day 1954, when I
first saw Gil Merrick play football for Birmingham City. I cannot
remember much about the day or indeed the game, but I do recall the
incredible feeling of being with over 33,000 people packed into St
Andrew's.

My dad took an old wooden beer crate for me to stand on, but it was
impossible to find a place on the terraces where you could be immune to
the swaying of the crowd as it moved with the tempo of the match.

I was passed down to the wall that surrounded the pitch where, along
with all the other young Brummies, mostly clad in short trousers, I was
amazed to be so close to the action and to be right behind the goal.

In our goal there was a giant bedecked in a green woollen jersey. He was
huge and seemed to fill the goal completely. That was my first impression
of Gil Merrick, St Andrew's and Birmingham City Football Club.

Needless to say, as Bluenoses will understand, we lost the game 1–0 to
Nottingham Forest, but to this day I still feel the same feeling of optimism,
expectation and camaraderie as I finally reach my plastic seat in the Tilton
Road end, now at the age of 61.

I first met Gil Merrick on 2 March 2004 when he was guest of honour
at my Bluenose Executive Lunch Club meeting at the China Red cantonese
restaurant in Broad Street, Birmingham. Everyone turned up to meet the
most influential person in the history of Birmingham City Football Club.

Even though he was over 80 and a little unsteady on his feet, he kept us
all amused telling stories of his experiences as a footballer and a manager.
One of our members had brought his dad along as a guest, and he had
with him the book Gil had written in the early 1950s ready to ask for his

signature, but I realised that so much of what Gil had told us over lunch (his first experience of chinese food!) had happened after the publication of it that I thought a second book would be very worthwhile.

Gil's career stopped as soon as it had started with the outbreak of World War Two, and this book provides a vivid insight into the world of football at that time. As a player he kept goal on more than 700 occasions, which is still a record to this day, and as a manager his record is second to none in Birmingham City terms. Up to the present, 2009, he is still the only manager to win a major trophy – The Football League Cup in 1963. He played for England 23 times alongside all-time England heroes such as Stan Matthews, Nat Lofthouse, Billy Wright, Tom Finney, Jimmy Dickinson and Alf Ramsey.

It has been an immense pleasure to sit alongside this Birmingham City legend in the back lounge of his home in Shirley, Solihull, listening to the personal recollections from the man himself, and he is someone I now count as a friend.

Malcolm Page is a personal friend of mine and, typical of his unassuming nature, his response to my request for him to write this foreword was 'Why me?' His initial draft was a little short and when I asked him why his reply was, 'I didn't want to put too much in about me'. As you have just read, I finally got him to appreciate that his career was a reflection of Gil's personality and management style and that he was important!

Malcolm played for the Blues for almost 17 years before moving to Oxford in February 1981, making 394 senior appearances. He gained Welsh International honours at every level before earning 28 full caps.

Keith Dixon

FOREWORD
by Malcolm Page

*'A man without loyalty does not exist. It stirs and arouses him, brings meaning,
direction and purpose into his life and unifies his
activities in both thought and action.'*

The first time I saw Gil Merrick was on a Bush 15in black and white television in the back room of my auntie and uncle's house in mid-Wales. My father and I were invited as a treat to watch the 1956 FA Cup Final at Wembley and this was the only TV for miles and miles. I was nine years old and this was the first football match that I can remember watching – 12 months later my father took me to my first 'live' match, and I was shocked to discover that these events were actually in colour!

Goalkeeping was my thing at the time and the strikingly handsome figure of Birmingham City's 'keeper had a great impact on me. Why goalkeeping? I lived with my parents in a 200-year-old cottage on an estate on the Welsh border. One side of the cottage had a massive stone chimney, and built onto that was a shed with a corrugated sloping roof. Every day after school I spent hours throwing a tennis ball against the stone chimney, allowing it to drop onto the roof which would divert the ball left or right meaning I had to react immediately, making saves to the left and right.

I followed Gil's career with interest on the wireless and, as all youngsters did, built up a fantasy about my favourite player. BBC's sports report on Saturdays at 5 o'clock was the weekly must, and in my mind I saw him stopping the goals being scored.

The second time I saw Gil was on a Saturday morning in the canteen at the school I attended in Wales. He was sitting there having a cup of tea. I was 15 years of age, playing for the county team, and he was manager of

Birmingham City Football Club. He was with his chief scout, Don Dorman, and although I had hoped their interest was in me, they did not speak directly to me that day.

My father was a well-known local referee at the time and helped out whenever one was needed; he was referee for that county game and he was always concerned that the players never knew I was his son. I got injured and was down on the ground nursing a sore ankle with a group of lads around me when the 'ref' came over and said, 'Are you alright son?' Immediately I responded, 'Yes dad!'

The third time that I saw Gil was in his office at St Andrew's in 1962, three months later, as I signed as an apprentice player with the Blues under the watchful eye of my father.

My father and I had travelled down to Birmingham on the Midland Red bus No. 192 from Ludlow to Navigation Street and were met by Gil in his big Ford Zephyr with bench front seat and column gear change. Don Dorman would slide back and forth on the front seat explaining where we were as we weaved around the city. We were then shown around St Andrew's and visited the Elmdon training ground.

It was agreed that the start of apprentice duties would be delayed because my parents had booked a holiday, so it was late July when I was again met in Navigation Street by the big Ford car and 'The Manager'. He drove me to my 'digs' at No. 42 Bray's Road, Sheldon, where I stayed for 10 years with Mr & Mrs Herbert and 'don't touch the dog' Bryn. My weekly rent was £3 15s, which was paid for by the club.

It was the start of my football career, and those two years working with Gil Merrick had a massive impact on how I approached not only my next 20 years in football but the rest of my life.

When I started my apprentice duties with the Blues, Gil treated us all with the same respect as the senior players – we were treated as adults and responded as such. The duties of apprentices at that time included helping the groundsman prepare the pitch, sweeping the terraces after matches and cleaning senior players' boots. It was in the boot room that we had the opportunity to talk with the manager, and this was where our respect for this man took root with all of us. Even now when I clean my golf shoes after a round I can still hear his 'Brummie' voice in my ear!

In 1964 Gil decided to offer me terms as a full professional, and my mother and father were invited to his office at St Andrew's to watch me sign. Rumours abounded at that time about huge incentives being offered to parents as an encouragement! I had already told my father that Johnny Vincent's folks had been given a fridge, and as the details of the contract were read out before I signed my father made a last-ditch attempt to provide mum with a present, asking, 'Is there anything else?' However, Gil did not offer any inducement. After the signing Gil took us to the Princess café on the Coventry Road for some fish'n'chips then back to the ground for the first-team match.

My weekly wage increased from £7 to £11 as a full professional, which was wonderful until Gil said, 'Of course you will be required to pay your digs money from now on!' So I had made '5 bob' – Thanks Gil!

From the thrill of being told you had cleared the first hurdle in the grand national of your football career, I was then to experience one of the saddest days of my life shortly after. Gil was told that the club did not require his services any more. What for? Well all I knew was what he had given the Blues, the fans, my family and me. How could the boot room ever be the same? It taught me the lesson that loyalty and commitment can bring disappointment.

'It is how you respond to that disappointment which I believe marks out a man of dignity and guts.'

For a period of time I followed Gil via the local press as he made his way into local football and commercial management. The one thing that stood out was his outstanding service to the company he worked for, and I often thought they must have had a wonderful 'boot room'!

The fourth time Gil turned up in my life was to attend my testimonial match 15 years later at St Andrew's. His being there meant the world to me because he had not been back since his sacking. I knew how tough it was for him to return after that disappointment, and I would like to think we were both 'rewarded' in some way that day.

This foreword contains my personal views on Gil Merrick; however, whenever I attend reunion celebrations it is obvious my affection and respect for him is shared with others. To see the respect and loyalty that former players have for this man is incredible; for example, when I see 'the team' they ask 'how is he?', and when I see Gil he asks 'how are the lads?'

'The philosopher Josiah Royce said that loyalty was the supreme moral good, and that one's devotion to an object mattered more than the merits of the object itself.'

Gil did not suffer fools gladly and was not afraid to make a hard decision; his loyalty was to a person or group of people, an ideal, a duty and the cause.

Gil was the goalkeeper in one of the most memorable international matches ever played at Wembley when Hungary beat England 6–3. It was seen as the match that signified England no longer dominated their continental rivals. Their most famous player was Ferenc Puskas, who scored a famous goal past Gil in the match. Two years ago Gil and I attended a signing session at the Sports Memorabilia event held at the Birmingham NEC. The organiser thought it would be a nice gesture to present to Gil a MicroStars model of Mr Puskas. Nice idea? Gil pointedly refused the gift!

I am so very much looking forward to reading his book, as I know many others will be. Gil has always retained a very private view of his life and experiences so the opportunity to read the inside story for the first time is intriguing.

I am proud and honoured to have been asked to write about this man, who has shown courage and above all loyalty not only to 'his team', his club, his company and his country but in his personal life as well.

Thanks Gil for the massive impact you have had on my life and the enriching experiences you gave to me and many others.

'Loyalty cannot be blueprinted. It cannot be produced on an assembly line. In fact, it cannot be manufactured at all, for its origin is the human heart – the centre of self-respect and human dignity.'

Maurice R. Franks

CHAPTER ONE
The End

Gil Merrick's association with Birmingham City Football Club ended when he was sacked as manager on 30 April 1964. Forty-five years later, football clubs are still firing managers with impunity, with little regard for loyalty and the need to have a long-term view about building a football team.

In discussing the format of this book with Gil, he was adamant that he wanted to start with his sacking. When I asked him why, he replied, 'I had no idea that I would be sacked, my record was good. Inter-Cities Fairs Cup Final and semi-final, League Cup winners, and I had kept us in the top division. Nobody has done better than me since, it was the worst thing and totally unexpected.'

So, let's go back to the late 1950s, as Gil recalls the whole affair.

It all started, I guess, when I was 38 years old. Although physically fit with probably two or three years left in me as a player, I knew that I had to be mentally fit to be a goalkeeper as you can not afford any mistakes! This being the case, I made my decision and informed Pat Beasley that I would be finishing at the end of the season.

Following the conclusion of the 1958–59 season, I received a letter from the club saying my services were no longer required, and it was signed by Pat Beasley. It really shook me up that after all the time I had been at the club I should receive such a letter.

I went to see the chairman, Harry Morris, who I was on good terms with, at his offices in Small Heath. When I showed him the letter he said he knew nothing about it and I believed him, even though as chairman of the club you would have thought he would have been aware of it. He made me promise not to go to the newspapers and confirmed that I would not be leaving Birmingham City football club as he wanted me to look after the reserves for 12 months to see how I got on in management. This eased my mind as I had a family to support and had already turned down one offer from my wife's uncle, who was on the board of Barrow Football Club. I had received a written offer to become their player-manager but I had turned it down because I do not believe in player-manager roles, particularly when it involves being a goalkeeper.

It was the September of the 1959–60 season when we were playing West Ham United reserves away – in those days the reserves kicked-off early so that the home club did not have the expense of floodlighting. The first team were playing Leicester at home and had been beaten badly, 3–4. The team included Schofield, Farmer, Sissons, Watts, Smith, Neal, Hellawell, Gordon, Stubbs, Orritt and Hooper. As the players were getting changed, David Wiseman, the director in charge of the reserves that day, said, 'They've lost again, you'll be playing next week.'

I was worried because if that was true I had not done any training and had had no pre-season, so I was rusty to say the least. When I got back to Birmingham I told Ken Fish (the first-team trainer) that I was back playing for the first team the following Saturday and he nearly fell to the floor in disbelief. Once he had got over it I asked him to help me get ready for playing first-team football again, and being the sort of bloke he was he met me every evening that week after I had finished at Greenmore College where I worked at the time – he worked me hard until I felt right.

My reappearance was against Burnley, a top side in those days, on 26 September 1959 at Turf Moor. As I was getting myself ready in the dressing room the director in charge, Harry Dare, sat by me and said, 'I don't fancy your chances today.' I was flabbergasted. He had never been a great motivator but what a thing to say to someone in my position. In the end we lost 3–1 but

I thought I played well. I played again the following week against Leeds United, which was John Charles's last game before his move to Italy. We won that one 2–0 with goals from Jimmy Barrett and Brian Taylor.

The following Wednesday I went to Brussels for an Inter-Cities Fairs Cup semi-final first-leg match against Union St Gilloise on 7 October. We won 4–2 in front of a crowd of 20,000. The team included Merrick, Sissons, Farmer, Watts, Smith, Neal, Hooper, Gordon, Orritt, Barrett and Taylor.

I was beginning to get back to normal when I contracted the flu so badly that Dr Gregory, the club doctor, declared me unfit for the next game. John Schofield came back and kept the position for the remainder of the season.

I was looking forward to another season when, in May 1960, while I was enjoying the school holidays from Greenmore College, I got a call to go to Olton golf club to meet certain directors on the course. Eventually I caught up with David Wiseman and his son Jack (currently president of Birmingham City Football Club) on the fourth green for them to announce, 'We'd like you to take over as manager of BCFC.' It was a dream come true!

Two days later, at the Beaufort Cinema in Stechford, which they owned, I attended a board meeting and I was officially offered the job, replacing Pat Beasley. I was over the moon. I resigned my position at Greenmore College and they gave me a wonderful send-off.

I did not inherit a great side. Blues staved off relegation by bringing back Peter Murphy at 37 years of age for the last seven games, in which he scored four goals. We won four, drew one and lost two, finishing 19th in Division One, so the side was struggling to hold its own before I was in charge.

In my first season, 1960–61, I had a very depleted squad. During the close season we had lost Jimmy Barrett, Billy Hume and Peter Murphy, and during the first half of the 1960–61 season we lost Gordon Astall, Johnny Gordon and Don Weston. I had no money to buy players but we got off to a good start anyway, drawing 2–2 at Bolton and then beating the Albion 2–1 at The

Hawthorns. We finished unbeaten in August, drawing with Sheffield Wednesday and completing the double over the Baggies. At the end of the season we were 19th again, just missing the drop to Division Two, but I had blooded some great young players: Winston Foster, Terry Hennessey, Colin Withers, Billy Rudd and Malcom Beard.

In the summer of 1961 I was on a cricket tour in Dorset playing, as was usual, for Clifford Coombs's Sports & Utilities side. We chatted about the situation at the club and because he believed I was having a difficult time he offered to donate £75,000 to the club as a transfer fund. At the next board meeting the directors were very concerned about any ulterior motives he might have, but I explained that he was doing it as a friend to both the club and myself. They agreed to accept the donation and with that money I was able to buy Jimmy Bloomfield, Bertie Auld, Jimmy Harris and Ken Leek. The proceeds of the sale of Dick Neal and Brian Orritt to Middlesbrough added £47,000 to the coffers, and we had the beginnings of a real team. The final piece of the jigsaw to me was the signing of a consistent goalscorer, so I bought Alex Harley.

In 1959–60, while I was looking after the reserves, it was suggested that I visit Barcelona with Ken Fish to observe Spanish football for a couple of weeks. It was a real eye-opener and so different to the way we did things in England. I was so impressed I requested that Emilio Aldecoa come back to England with us, which suited him because his wife was a nurse from Stafford.

Emilio was employed to train the youngsters and was one of the nicest fellows I have met in football. So, that was the management team: Ken Fish, Tom Smith looking after the reserves, Emilio with the youngsters, and me. Initially there was no interference from the board, I simply went to the board meetings to discuss team performance as an item on the agenda, but after a while their performance was the agenda! Later on it was suggested that Don Dorman, who was chief scout, should be appointed as my assistant. I should have refused at that time because I am convinced he became David Wiseman's spy in my camp!

We were playing Sheffield United on Saturday 25 May 1964 and needed a win to stay up which we did, winning 3–0. As I had been given three years to build a team, I felt I was making progress, but I had a funny feeling after the game when I went into the dressing room. The players were relieved and happy, and David Wiseman was there saying, 'Well done' and being overly enthusiastic with the backslapping. Alex Harley was also in the dressing room, although he had not played for the first team since the end of February. He said something about him not playing, to which Wiseman replied in a knowing way, 'It will be different for you next season.' Wiseman then told Don Dorman to get more champagne for the players, while I was left feeling isolated and as if I had had nothing to do with our escape from relegation.

The following Monday the office girl at St Andrew's asked me to go to the board room. When I got there they were all assembled: David Wiseman, Len Morris, Sam Richards and Walter Adams the secretary. David Wiseman opened up with, 'As we haven't made much progress we are getting rid of you.' There was no further explanation, no praise for the job I had done, and so I replied, 'OK if that's what you want.' It was as brief as that. I left the room, cleared my desk and left. I said farewell to Ken Fish and a few of the players. The FA Cup Final defeat had been bad enough, but my sacking and the manner of it broke my heart.

Ever since I started as a 17-year-old I had wanted to be the manager, and as the manager I had seen youngsters establish themselves and had also brought in experienced professionals, but in a few minutes it was all over for me. I got six months' pay and the company car but nothing made up for the disappointment – it took me two years to get over it.

I felt that the directors during my time at Blues were split equally in terms of those beneficial to the club and those only interested in what the club could do for them. There was Harry Morris, Len Morris and Harry Dare who were good for the club, while I considered that Bill Dare, Sam Richards and David Wiseman (whose son, Jack, and grandson, Michael, are both members of the Birmingham FC board today) were only really interested in what the club could do for them. Bill Camkin, who resigned early when I was still playing, was my idea of a top-class football club director. He loved the game and the club.

I never had a proper relationship with David Wiseman, and, although I do not know for certain, I think he resented the fact that I always dealt with the chairman Len Morris. Even though that was the right thing to do, it could have caused resentment from David Wiseman.

The manner in which I was sacked from the manager's job in June 1964 resulted in me disassociating myself from the club for nearly 40 years. The nature of my sacking was in my opinion conducted as an act of revenge by David Wiseman, who had held a grudge against me since the early 1950s. When it had been announced that I was to make my debut for England, David Wiseman approached me and said, 'Gil, I've got the first caps of Harry Hibbs and Joe Bradford and I want yours too.' I refused, saying my first cap was going to my father, and I don't think David Wiseman ever forgave me for that and he was delighted to give me my termination letter.

CHAPTER TWO
The Beginning

I t was inevitable that I would devote my football career to Birmingham City as I was the third generation of Merricks to have a link with the club. My grandfather helped in the building of the St Andrew's ground when he was working for a haulage firm that were engaged in the job of filling in the huge quarry on which the stadium was built.

My dad played for Birmingham Boys at Muntz Street, which was the Blues ground from 1878 to 1883. It was not the greatest of grounds, as the playing surface was rather bumpy, which annoyed a lot of visiting teams. Later he played at St Andrew's as a semi-professional goalscoring inside-forward for Nuneaton and Worcester City. And then, of course, there was me.

As a nipper of six I was always waiting for my dad to come home to Shakespeare Street, Sparkhill, from his work as a sheet metal worker so that the Brummie derby could begin!

Dad would play for Villa (he was a Villa fan) and I would play for Birmingham in our nightly game in my mother's back kitchen. After he had washed and shaved I would hurry him into the kitchen to play the game, where we would both defend a door from either a tennis ball or a squashed-up ball of paper. We had all sorts of rules: if it went in off the stove or the boiler it was a no goal and anyone who drove the ball under the sink gave away a free-kick. The match would go on for about an hour before mom threw us out of the kitchen.

It was my dad who gave me the soccer bug, he taught me how to kick a football with my instep so that it went half the length of the garden. Not bad for a four-year-old! The first Christmas present I can remember was a pair of football boots and a 'caser' (a genuine leather football).

At the age of seven we moved to Fenton Road, Acocks Green, which was about the time my dad started taking me to Villa Park and I became a Villan! Fenton Road was an ideal spot for a football nut like myself. Behind the house was the field that became my childhood playground. Having the field less than a goal-kick away from my garden was like living in a football ground, and it cost my family and my neighbours 3d per week to hire it! Nothing else interested me. I would rush home from school, gobble down my tea and race out onto the field. There was always someone out to get a game with, and if my mates were not out there were always adults around just as keen to play.

Although I was football mad there was the occasional distraction like a fishing trip for 'jackbannacks', bird-nesting hunts and collecting conkers, but they were rare distractions from football. Other lads wanted to be train drivers or firemen, but for me Ted Sagar was my hero and I had no other thought than becoming a footballer, and in particular a goalkeeper.

So keen was I that one Christmas I was given a green goalkeeper's jersey and the lads teased me by shouting, 'Here comes Harry' because Harry Hibbs was the hero of the time for Birmingham and England. Little did my mates know that I would follow in his footsteps!

It was always my choice to be in goal. In other teams it was often the position given to the player with the least ability or the quietest one, so this, therefore, made me popular with my friends as usually no one wanted to get between the sticks (or jumpers). But I was literally born to be a 'keeper, you only had to look at my hands to realise that!

We formed a team called Fenton Rovers and organised games against other roads and scratch sides from the local area. Out of the Fenton Road team there was only one other player who became a professional – Albert Clutterbuck who played full-back for Blues before moving on to be the trainer at Moor Green FC.

I was nine when I first played for the school junior side – Acocks Green in the South Birmingham Schools League. I must have been a fairly hefty lad for my age because the senior master Mr Vaughan wanted me in the senior side and the junior football master Mr Mason insisted I stayed with him. I eventually moved to the seniors when I was 11 years old, playing with boys two or three years older than me, and I am pleased to say that we won the local Victoria Shield for the only time in the school's history. Mr Mumford, an official of the Schools' FA, presented us with the Victoria Shield after the match, saying, 'You've seen a goalkeeper this evening who will surely wear the England jersey one day.'

Mr Vaughan gave me my first coaching tip: 'Whatever you do, keep your hands warm; it is one thing a goalkeeper must always remember.' Funnily enough during my career I only ever wore woollen gloves when it was wet!

Twelve months later I received my first football instruction. I was chosen to play in a trial for South Birmingham Schoolboys – we got two days off school for a training get-together which included exercises and practice. Mr Mumford was in charge, and I remember him telling me to learn to kick the ball dead off the ground instead of letting the full-back flick the ball to me so that I could kick it from my hands. 'One day they will do away with that co-operation with the full-back,' he suggested. It was an outstanding piece of advice and I practised hard at dead-ball kicking. How right he was as the rule was eventually changed.

At the age of 12 I was selected for my first representative match for South Birmingham against Stafford in the English Schools Trophy. At that time in the local sports shop there was a wonderful pair of shin pads; they were beautiful and lined in lovely thick lambs' wool but incredibly expensive at five shillings! I must have mentioned it to my folks because when I told them that I had been chosen for South Birmingham they said, 'We'll buy you those pads.' It is worth mentioning that I wore those same pair of pads throughout my football career in every match and they were in nearly as good condition when I hung up my boots as they were in 1934. My mom, Helen, was a housewife and she knitted my football socks for me – blue and white hoops of course!

When I was playing for South Birmingham Schools there was another 'keeper, Alan Wakeman, who played for North Birmingham Schools. He was a year older than me but had stayed on at school for another year, and he got picked for England Schoolboys. If he had left school I would probably have got picked for Schoolboy honours instead. He was an outstanding youngster but never quite maintained that standard into adulthood, although he turned professional with Aston Villa before joining Doncaster Rovers after the war. I met Alan some years later when he was manager of Bilston Town.

Immediately on leaving school I signed my first football form. I had my leaving certificate and a school report that stated, 'outstanding at sport'. As I went through the gate onto the pavement I was approached by Mr Williams from Shirley Juniors, which was the finest local junior club and widely recognised as a nursery for Birmingham City. He asked me if I would like to play for them and I agreed immediately. He told me to come down on the next Friday night for training, and I was on top of the world.

Shirley Juniors was a progressive club run by Arthur 'Slogger' Williams and Harry Smith. It was well organised and club members had to conform to a laid down form of discipline. Every Friday night we had an hour's PT under the control of Harry Smith, but there was no coaching or tuition in the soccer arts. I stayed with Shirley for half a season and then left. With so many players at the club I had no chance of getting a regular place in the team.

I joined a couple of my mates at Olton Sports for two seasons. I had still to receive any official coaching so was virtually self-taught. If I found goals being scored against me were through a mistake on my part, I changed my style or technique in an effort to overcome the fault. Towards the end of my second season with Olton we played Shirley Juniors in a cup match and afterwards they asked me to go back – which I did.

The following season, aged 16, Mr Williams asked me sign amateur forms for Birmingham City. It was not the exciting moment I had hoped for; nothing was said about if or when I would play for any of the Birmingham sides. In fact, they did not run a junior team at that time. It was just like signing for any junior league club. I discovered years later that Blues denied any knowledge of ever having had me on amateur forms. I never got to the bottom of it but it may well have been a way for Mr Williams to keep me at Shirley Juniors.

In August 1939 junior professional clubs in the Birmingham area were holding their usual pre-season trials, and I came across an advertisement for a new club, Solihull Town, who were entering the Birmingham Combination League. Their manager was the ex-Blues full-back Ned Barkas and he agreed for me to have a trial in an evening match. I had had a decent game when I was approached by a local newspaper photographer, Tom Fraser, who told me, 'I've been told to tell you don't sign for anybody'. While I was changing word came through that Ned Barkas wanted me to sign for Solihull Town. This confused me, bearing in mind Tom Fraser's message. I decided to leave the ground and not talk to anyone.

Walter Taylor, Blues' chief scout and assistant manager, takes up the story: 'The first time I saw Gil play was in the South Birmingham side in the English Schools Trophy – in about 1936 I should think. I saw him twice more soon after that playing for Shirley Juniors and on every occasion I thought he was a useful player. In those days we did not have junior teams at Birmingham City, and therefore did not put youngsters on the books. However, I made a mental note of him, even though it got tucked a long way back in my mind. It was a couple of years or so later, in fact the late summer of 1939, that I arranged a Birmingham trial at The Moorlands [the Moor Green ground] before the start of the season. One of the goalkeepers I had selected cried off the day before the trial. I spent a harassing morning wondering what I should do, and at lunch time, walking down Bordesley Green East near the Blues' ground, I bumped into a lad named Jim Askill who played with Gil for Shirley Juniors. Immediately he reminded me of Gil – just the man I want, I thought to myself. I told Askill what I had in mind, but he shattered me by saying, "I think you're too late; I think he's signed for Solihull Town. Anyway he's playing for them in a trial tomorrow night." Nevertheless, I took Gil's address from Jim and went out to his home in Acocks Green. His father saw me when I got out there and when I told him the reason for my visit said, "You've had him once and didn't bother, and anyway you're too late now – he's playing for Solihull Town tomorrow." But has he signed for them? I wanted to know. "Not yet," said his father, "but he will after the match." There and then I put a proposition to his father. Would he agree to Gil not signing for anyone else if I promised to sign him as a professional for Birmingham after the game? His father thought that was fair and so we parted on the strength of a gentleman's agreement. In the meantime I managed to find someone to fill the gap in the Birmingham trial and on the following night I was at Solihull Town to see their trial match. After the game had been going on for 10 minutes, I was hot and cold all over in quick succession. I was never more certain in my life that Gil Merrick was great and would make the grade. He was better than I had imagined; he had come on so much more than I could have expected. But what sent shivers through me was that I knew Ned Barkas and George

Featherstone of Solihull would realise how good he was and would do everything in their power to persuade him to sign for them; after all, they held the edge since he was there at their invitation. The only thing I could do was ask Tom Fraser to speak to Gil and tell him not to sign for anyone. Even then I was worried stiff in case Fraser put the message over in earshot of club officials. The next move was to try and see Gil alone. My friend George Swain was at the game with me and we waited in the lane that runs outside the ground knowing that Gil would be almost certain to come that way. It was an agonising wait, wondering whether he had been persuaded to sign. Eventually he came along with some of his teammates, and because I knew they might recognise me I asked George Swain to have a word with Gil and tell him a gentleman wanted to speak to him at the corner of the shops on the Stratford Road. Well Gil came over, said he hadn't signed and had left it to his father. I told him what we had in mind and he said that I should see his father the next day. The next morning his father was as good as his word and I signed Gil for Birmingham. I heard then that Solihull had done everything they could in a bid to get his signature. In fact, had they signed him, they could have transferred him to Huddersfield the next day for a good fee. It was one of the most worrying jobs I've ever had because I knew others must have realised on the night of the trial how good a proposition Merrick was. It was one of my luckiest shots in 30 years of scouting. If I had not met Jim Askill in the street that morning I would not have thought of Merrick until I read of his signing for someone else, and I would certainly not have got him if his father had not kept his word.'

As a youngster I had supported Aston Villa with great interest and enthusiasm and, chiefly, because my father went to Villa Park regularly after his playing career ended. Although I nursed a secret hope to sign for Villa, my father agreed to my joining Blues for two good reasons: it was a real chance of becoming a professional and at the same time I could also continue in my job as an apprentice sheet metal worker. I was given a £5 signing-on fee, but that was only 50 per cent of it – I got the other half years later! So with £3 10s a week from football, plus £2 a week from my job, I was a prosperous young man.

For my first game I needed a basic goalkeeper's kit of a pair of gloves and a cap. Gloves were no problem, but as I had not worn a cap since my schooldays this was proving more difficult to acquire. Fortunately my father's favourite headgear was an ordinary peaked civilian cap and he gave me one of his old ones on the morning of the match. It is a strange fact that I wore that cap for that first game but never wore it again, although for years and years I simply carried it with me. I chose not to wear a cap because I preferred to get used to the glare of the sun without one because at some point in a game, when going for a high ball, the sun would come below the peak level and the sudden dazzle could result in a serious error. That cap became part of my uniform and it was a good place to keep my gloves. Over the years it became battered and dirty, and lost all its shape and strength such that I could not have worn it even if I had wanted to. Eventually it was stolen in Argentina by a little kid who ran behind the goal, grabbed it and was away into the crowd before I knew it was missing. That match was abandoned at 0–0 and I got a replacement cap from dad. I have always loathed to get rid of my old equipment: my cap survived the wartime fire at St Andrew's, my shin guards had been with me since I was 11 and a pair of boots would be worn until they fell apart.

My first Blues outing was for the A team against Wolverhampton Wanderers in the Birmingham Combination at Jack Mould's ground. The boy who led the Wolves that day and scored twice against me was 15-year-old Billy Wright, under whose captaincy I would make all of my England appearances.

The teams were:

Blues: Merrick, Parr, Galley, Bartlett, R.E. Foulkes, Harper, Lamas, Massart, W. Pears, Graham, Southam.

Wolves: Elliott, Robinson, Brown, Hipkins, Bainbridge, Rawcliffe, Marshall, Thoms, Wright, Hocks, Steen.

I name the teams chiefly to prove what a tremendous gamble the whole business of junior development is. These were the third teams of Blues and Wolves, hand-picked young men whom it was thought would make their mark. But did it happen? Foulkes captained Walsall and Norwich, Massart played for the Blues, Walsall, Bury and Chesterfield and then there was myself who reached League football out of the Blues side. For Wolves, Elliott went to Chester and Steen and Wright played first-team football for the club.

Blues lost that game 3–1. George Blackburn, later senior kit man at Blues, was looking after the side and said to me, 'What happened to you over the first goal?' I told him I thought the ball was going out, which was why I had stood and watched it as it curled into the net, to which he replied, 'You don't want to think it's always better to make sure.' I can truthfully say that was one of the very few, perhaps even the first, real pieces of advice I had received.

On the following Monday I was up at the ground training in the evening, wondering if I would be picked for the next A game on the coming Wednesday. I asked George Blackburn if he knew the team and he told me not to be concerned as I would not be in it! This really dented my confidence – I had been dropped right at the start of my career.

A short time later war broke out and in less than a month my youthful hopes were sent crashing down. It was nearly a year before I played serious football again, being lent out to Sutton Town.

Later I played for Blues reserves in 'friendly' games and when there was no match I played as a 'guest' for other clubs. I played three times for the Albion and once for Nottingham Forest with Cyril Trigg and J. Bye. I also guested for Northampton Town with Frank Mitchell and Don Dearson.

All this before I had made my Blues first-team debut – I was on my way.

CHAPTER THREE
The Player

Why a goalkeeper? I think it lies within me being defensively minded, as it does not matter what sport I am playing I always favour defence. I am a baseline tennis player, defensive at table tennis and a defence interceptor at basketball, being sufficiently talented enough to win while representing my command in the army.

My big chance to prove myself came at the end of the 1939–40 season. While continuing with my apprenticeship and training at the ground twice a week, I was told by Sam Richards, the club secretary, that I was playing for the first team in the evening match the following day.

---

v Leicester City (h), 20 May 1940   **Drew 0–0**

Blues: Merrick, Quinton, Hughes, Bye, Foulkes, Harris, Jones, Gardner, Trigg, Bodle, Moss.

Attendance: 1,500

While it was only a wartime regional match, to me it was just like a big League game. I was 18 years old and the Blues team included many great pre-war players. I worked all day at the factory but left an hour early, and the lads loved that and 'hammered' me out, banging on their benches with their hammers!

I kept my place in the team and became a regular the following season, making 13 appearances. Now I began to learn about the game. My education came about as a result of match experience but also from listening and joining in with the discussions about tactics and positional play with the likes of W.A. 'Bill' Camkin the club's honorary wartime manager, Arthur Turner, Fred Harris, Don Dearson, Billy Hughes, Wilson Jones, Dennis Jennings…these were the men who showed me the right road. It was about natural ability and a willingness to learn from your experiences.

A goalkeeper does not require the same intensive training that was part of my colleagues' preparation. Lapping the pitch or running over Elmdon Park was never a necessity for me but sprinting was vital. I emphasise sprinting because it is agility that counts for so much in goalkeeping. To help develop agility and quickness of the eye there is no better training than taking part in such ball games as basketball and table tennis and particularly small ball games like skittleball and hand ball. Naturally I got plenty of exposure to these games during the PE and games sessions I had to organise at Greenmore College as Sports Master.

Keeping fit was a self-discipline for me and, of course, when I was not at the training ground I was in a tracksuit at school getting involved, I was never one of those PE teachers that sat around watching the pupils without breaking into a sweat. My regular training routine certainly paid dividends as my playing record shows I missed very few games through injury, which often caused comment from the reserve team goalkeepers, Jack Wheeler and Johnny Schofield, whose first-team appearances were severely restricted due to my consistency of play and fitness. Poor Jack had also deputised for Harry Hibbs so he had had to play second fiddle on two occasions.

I would have found it incredibly difficult to be continually in the reserves because you need to playing at the highest possible level as often as possible to keep your skills and concentration at their peak. The modern way of rotating a squad would never have suited me, as either a player or a manager,

I believe in playing your best team in every game, regardless of the importance of the match.

The key ingredients to being a good footballing side are ability, fitness, concentration and tactics, which initially come from the manager, who, if he has any sense, takes advice from his senior players.

Corners are a major area for tactics and for massive input from the goalkeeper. When Blues defended corners we would have Jeff Hall off the line and within striking distance of the opposing left-winger, thus ensuring every man was marked before the kick was taken. This was contrary to the way most of our opponents set up for corners. Instead they would have the right-back standing behind the keeper, beyond the far post, as the winger prepared to take the corner, and as the goalkeeper moved towards the ball, the right-back would slip into position on the goalline, a yard or two from the post. On one occasion we changed our tactics in a game against Tottenham Hotspur in the sixth round of the FA Cup second replay at Wolverhampton on 9 March 1953. Both Jeff and Ken Green were on the line, and there was a very good reason for our change of tactics. In the first two games against Spurs, Ken Green had closely marked the Spurs right-winger, Sonny Walters, for left wing corners, because I knew both the Spurs wingers made a practice of running round the back of the defence to meet corners in an unorthodox surprise move. We found out in the first two ties that this move was not, in fact, so dangerous as the lofted corners hit just outside the six yard line for their forwards Bennett and Duquemin, who were particularly good in the air. They were going up against Ray Ferris in the air, and trying to head the ball through in the angles of the woodwork. Duquemin succeeded with this tactic in the first replay at White Hart Lane, heading home from a Les Medley corner from among a group of players about eight yards out, inches inside the post. As a result of this we decided to bring Ken back on the line to check the danger of these headers near the posts, and we arranged for our left-winger, Billy Wardle, to come back and mark Walters in the penalty area, while his fellow winger Medley was taking corner kicks. When it was Walter's turn to take corners then our right-winger, Jackie Stewart, came back and marked Medley. This could have perhaps been the start of midfielders tracking back to help out their defenders, which is so much part of the modern game in the 21st century. Spurs did not succeed in scoring a goal against us from a corner in that third match, although we did lose 1–0 in front of 50,801 fans that day. The team was: Merrick, Hall, Green, Bannister, Badham, Boyd, Stewart, Purdon, Trigg, Ferris, Wardle.

I learnt all about calling for the ball and being assertive as a goalkeeper in the goal area from two very memorable events. I was playing a match for Albion at Wrexham, and 'Popeye' Jones was at centre-half when a high ball came across and I went out to gather it. I did not call because I did not know anything about such a thing at that time. As I jumped to catch the ball Jones came back attempting a header. He hit me on the top of the nose and knocked me out. I only have to look at the slightly misshapen top part of my nose to remind myself of that incident.

The second event occurred while I was playing for Blues against Derby County. I went up to take a high ball and Arthur Turner our centre-half went up with me. If I had called, Arthur would have prepared himself in case of a collision, but I did not and as I went to get the ball my knee caught Arthur in the back and he went out like a light. Almost immediately after the end of the game Dally Duncan, who was playing for Derby, came over to me and said, 'You silly stupid young man; you never said a word about it being your ball.' That is a cleaned-up version of what he said but even that was a mild rebuke compared to what Arthur said after he recovered – he really had a go at me, but it was for my own good.

And I learnt quickly!

If catching high balls is important to a goalkeeper's armoury of skills then saving penalties is crucial.

It was Portsmouth's hard-shooting forward, Duggie Reid, who was really responsible for me taking a detailed study of the whole subject of penalty taking and the possibilities of a goalkeeper saving penalty kicks. It was 5 January 1946 and Portsmouth were playing Blues in the FA Cup third round first leg at St Andrew's. Portsmouth were awarded a penalty and Reid took the kick, hitting the ball right-footed to my right, meaning I had to go full stretch just managing to punch the ball away so that it went out for a throw-in on the far side of the field. This was one of my best penalty saves and certainly the first I achieved in big time football as it was my FA Cup debut!

Up until then I had taken the line that it was sheer luck whether a goalkeeper saved a penalty or not, luck in the sense that a goalkeeper gambled on going the right way. Naturally I was pleased to have saved Reid's shot, and I felt particularly pleased because I had saved a ball going away from me, and at speed. In analysing what had happened I realised that from the angle Reid ran at the ball and the power with which he hit, he had no alternative but to hit the ball to my right. This set me thinking that if I studied a player's run-up and action in kicking the ball, rather than waiting for the ball in flight and depending on quickness of the eye to make a save, I would have a better chance of going the right way, which increased my chances of saving a penalty to one in two.

Jackie Stewart helped me in almost every aspect of goalkeeping. I practised for hours with him. I started by getting him to tell me which side he would put the ball and then watching his action when he shot. From there we advanced to him shooting without giving me any verbal indication of which side the ball would go and without being influenced in that way I could confirm in my own mind that I knew which way to dive. We must have gone over this literally hundreds of times, and possibly as a result of this practice there came a spell when Jackie was the club's number one penalty taker. Just as a side note, Jackie took two penalties in League games – and missed on both occasions! Perhaps having stopped so many of his shots, I had given him an inferiority complex!

This was never something that troubled me, in fact total confidence in one's ability is paramount to a goalkeeper, particularly when facing on-rushing forwards.

It was the fourth round of the 1950–51 FA Cup against Derby County at the Baseball Ground on 27 January 1951. A long through ball split our defence who at the time were square and well up behind our forwards. When the pass was made, McLaren, the Derby outside-left, was more than 35 yards from my goal. I had seen the danger in the move when the through pass was kicked, for McLaren was level with our right back, Jack Badham. It was clear that Jack was going to be beaten by the pass since he was too far away to intercept. Immediately, I had the confidence to start coming out fast at the same time as McLaren made his move towards the through ball. By confidently anticipating this I was able to make such an early start from the line that when McLaren got to the ball I was almost on him right at the angle of the penalty box. As a result he shot, barely being able to control the ball, and I was so near to him that the ball hit my chest and rebounded away to be cleared. We went onto to win that game 3–1 with Trigg, Stewart and Smith scoring. A crowd of 37,384 saw us advance into the fifth roundThe team was made up of: Merrick, Badham, Martin, Boyd, Atkins, Ferris, Stewart, Higgins, Trigg, Smith, Berry.

At the end of 1944 I finished my apprenticeship and was called up into the army. Only twice in the 18 months I was an infantryman with the Royal Warwickshire regiment did they persuade me to go into goal. On one occasion in an inter-battalion game I hurt my finger early on and had to switch to centre-half. I played a blinder! That defensive mentality again!

When I moved to Abergavenny I managed to convince them that I was a better centre-half than a goalkeeper except on the occasion the CO ordered me to play in goal in an inter-regiment fixture. I enjoyed playing out as it helped my fitness levels.

I joined the Army Physical Training Corps and eventually had my own gymnasium at Oswestry, which was the headquarters of the Mercian Brigade of Western Command.

While at Oswestry I began playing basketball seriously, which is great training for a goalkeeper because it demands very quick and clean handling of a ball plus you need the ability to throw the ball accurately. For months on a nightly basis I played basketball until I won army representative honours.

The army allowed me to play regularly for Blues and gave me a taste of the big match atmosphere. I played against the French army in Paris, the Belgian army in Brussels and against the BAOR in Germany, all top-class sides.

My days in the army finished the way they had started, with me playing in an outfield position – centre-forward! Keith Jones, who played for Villa and Wales, had come into Western Command and one day when we were short of a centre-forward for the Inter-Command Cup ties I suggested that I had a go. After doing well in a trial I led the line with Keith in goal against Southern Command at Shrewsbury. We won 2–1 and I scored both goals. The next game was against Eastern Command at Wrexham, and again we won 2–1 and again I scored twice. Walter Taylor was at the game and he shattered my ego in more ways than one by saying, 'I still think you would have made a good centre-half.'

I made my FA Cup debut on 5 January 1946 against Portsmouth when the competition was reinstated after the war. All the rounds up to the semi-final were played over two legs. We won 1–0 due to a Flewin own-goal in front of a crowd of 33,845.

v Portsmouth, 5 January 1946   Won 1–0

Blues: Merrick, Duckhouse, Jennings, Harris, Turner, Mitchell, Mulraney, Dougall, Jones, Bodle, Edwards.

Scorer: Flewin (og)
Attendance: 33,845

Competitive football began again at the end of August 1946, and to prepare for the new season Blues went on a pre-season tour of Switzerland.

George Edwards, Blues' Welsh international, described the tour in his article 'Climbed the Swiss Alps': The tour of Switzerland, undertaken by 14 players and eight officials, can be regarded as a complete success both from the social and playing points of view. Leaving London on Monday May 3rd after 24 hours travelling, we arrived at the Hotel Baren, Berne, our headquarters for nine days.

Here we were made thoroughly at home and enjoyed the luxury of every attention that could be given. Berne, the beautiful old capital of Switzerland, had an excellent shopping centre, containing lots of everything of which we had been starved for years, was 'torture' to all of us because of the acute franc shortage. We all resembled little boys at Christmas time who, with but a few pennies in their pockets, thoroughly scrutinise the goods on display before making the final plunge. Indeed this habit persisted throughout our wanderings in this foreign land. Our first coach tour of the trip ended with an official dinner at the White Horse Inn at Zäziwil and is chiefly remembered for the impromptu concert which followed when the city choir brought the audience to its feet with inspired renderings of the two numbers in the city choir's repertoire. The second tour to Lausanne saw most of the players grouped around a certain bronze statue by the lakeside. Gilbert Merrick and Cyril Trigg almost fell over themselves in their eagerness to obtain films to make a permanent record. [Gil recalls the bronze statue was of a naked lady!]

Other memorable occasions during the first part of the tour included the debut of Harold Bodle as a crooner in the Kursaal, a nightclub in the city. [Gil recalls that Bodle had a bloody good voice!]

In rather a different vein was our visit to the Tobler chocolate factory when, for a change, the boys were quite speechless. How could they speak when their mouths were full of freshly made chocolate?

From Berne we proceeded to Lucerne for a further seven days, during which tours were made to the Trummelbach Falls and the Tell country and games were played against Zurich and Lucerne. Outstanding events here included the efforts of keen golfers Fred Harris, Neil Dougall and Harold Bodle to keep out of the rough; the predicament of Ken Green and Fred Slater who found themselves in a sailing boat in the middle of Lake Lucerne and who had to blow their noses hard to create sufficient wind in order to return.

Yes, a successful tour with only one note of discord, for one member of the team thought fit to complain about being placed continually in the back row of the choir. It is understood, however, that for the next tour he has been promised promotion to the second row of the chorus. The results of the matches played were: La Chaux du Fonds won 3–2; Berne won 2–0; Basle won 5–0; Zurich (Young Fellows) drew 1–1; Lucerne won 1–0.

Gil remembers an incident on this tour involving Dennis Jennings.

A group of us went out in Berne one night. When all the street lamps came on, thousands of moths appeared attracted to the light. We were all slapping them to get rid of 'em – there were literally thousands. Anyway, Frank Mitchell, Cyril Trigg and Ted Duckhouse each caught a handful of these moths and took them back to the hotel. We crept upstairs to Dennis's room, opened the door and threw these moths in. Dennis nearly had a heart attack when, hearing the noise at the door, he switched on the light and found all these insects in his room. Harry Storer read us the riot act at breakfast the following morning.

Gil made his League debut on the opening day of the 1946–47 season in Division Two against Tottenham Hotspur playing away on 31 August 1946. He missed only one game that season, against Millwall on 17 May when his deputy was Bill Wheeler, who, due to Gil's consistency, only played 13 games during a 10-year stay at St Andrew's.

v Tottenham Hotspur, 31 August 1946	Won 2–1

Blues: Merrick, Dearson, Hughes, Harris, Duckhouse, Mitchell, Mulraney, Dougall, C.W. Jones, Bodle, Edwards.

Scorer: Jones (27)
Attendance: 51,256

Approximately 18 months before I was demobbed I came under the influence of Harry Storer, who did more for my career as a professional footballer than anyone else.

Harry was one of the greatest talkers on football, in fact just listening to him in his early days with the club made me realise how little I knew about the game. The lads loved to hear him talk. He had a host of football stories about people in the game, and he was always trying to keep you thinking about football.

On Tuesday mornings when we reported at the ground after the weekend game many has been the time when he would chat with the lads in the dressing room about the match. An argument would start about some particular point and he would walk out halfway through, leaving the lads to carry on a heated discussion that would not have started but for him.

He played cricket for Derbyshire for many years so when he fancied a change he would switch from football stories to cricket ones. I felt his stories always had a purpose, that there was always a message in there.

He hated cowards and shirkers, and anyone who was a bit shy in the tackle to him was a coward.

When we were waiting for transport to an away game he would look around the players and not count them but the number of hearts he was taking to the game – 'Only nine and a half hearts today, might be close.'

The secret to his success was his ability to put across tactical information, and the way he made the players have faith in him. It certainly worked as we won the Second Division Championship in the 1947–48 season. His man management and motivational skills were well ahead of his time.

He was constantly thinking about the game and coming up with new tactics. Since Harry had been manager of the club I had not dropped a ball in any game. For me and thankfully Harry that was one tactic we agreed on; that goalkeepers should whenever possible catch the ball cleanly and only when this is not an option should the ball be punched clear. In a match against Bury in season 1950–51 I came out for a high ball among a crowd of players. I was confident of catching it, though that was perhaps a time when I should have fisted it away. I half got the ball but in the jostling, lost it, and it ended up in the net. As it turned out we drew 3–3, but after the game I was feeling rather sorry for myself when Harry came along and in discussing the goal he said, 'If a goalkeeper catches eight out of every ten he goes for, he will be good enough for my team.' Perhaps he was being a little generous, but coming from a man who was not only a master of defence tactics but also demanded a high standard, it was an encouraging thought. The match was played on 20 January 1951 at St Andrew's in front of 26,000 spectators. The team was: Merrick, Hall, Martin, Boyd, Atkins, Ferris, Stewart, Rowley, Trigg, Higgins, Berry. The scorers that day were Trigg and Stewart.

Harry could make players feel that they were better than they were, he was a player's man and though he was hard and aggressive the lads knew he was for them 100 per cent. He made me realise that the only way to manage a club is for the boss to be fair and honest with players in everything. News travels fast in a dressing room and once the team loses faith then the rot sets in.

Harry could smell trouble and unrest a mile off, and once he sensed it he would deal with it. One season there was a problem with the players' wives not being guaranteed a seat for the games. The lads felt bad about it and there was lots of talk. Harry immediately called a meeting and made his feelings instantly clear: 'Wives and football don't mix', but even so he made sure arrangements were put in hand for organising seats for the women.

When I first joined the Blues there was a director, Mr Woolman, who was a nationally acclaimed chrysanthemum grower. He was around at the same time as Bill Camkin and they were both 100 per cent for Birmingham City Football Club. I remember on one return journey from Derby our driver got lost, no motorways in those days, so Mr Woolman got up alongside him and gave him directions, saying, 'I know the way'. The journey ended with the roof being taken off the coach under a low bridge!

Every pre-season the playing staff were invited to Mr Woolman's home in Knowle for a garden party. Obviously, being a keen gardener, his grounds were fantastic and even included a boating lake. This particular year, which was only my second, our visit coincided with the local church fête so the various sideshows and games were still available to us. One of the stalls was a shooting target game with air guns and pellets. Jimmy Dailey was having a go when suddenly he shouted, 'Indians!' and shot at a bowler hat that was passing by on the other side of a 5ft hedge. It must have been at least 50 yards and he hit it, and the bowler hat and its wearer slipped from view with the cry, 'I've been shot!' It was the head gardener. Everyone ran over to him and he had been hit very close to one of his eyes. Later at the local hospital it became evident that he was very close to losing his eye.

Mr Woolman, who was normally a quiet man, unceremoniously kicked us out and that was the last time we were invited to his home. When we got onto the coach to leave, the music on the radio was *Shotgun Boogie*. Mr Woolman was a real gent and when I won my first international cap he named a chrysanthemum after me.

During a career that spanned many years and 551 appearances, Gil played up against some of the great players of the era. From his early days he came up against some amazing opponents:

Every goalkeeper has his own idea about which forwards he regards as most dangerous – the men he must watch most carefully. Thinking back on players I have met, three names come readily to mind – Trevor Ford, Doug Reid and Len Shackleton. I would say without hesitation that Ford was the most difficult forward I have ever played against. He never let a goalkeeper rest or take his time in clearing a ball. He was always challenging and harassing, and unless a goalkeeper has great powers of concentration and confidence in himself he was likely to fumble the ball or take his eyes off it. I rate Doug Reid of Portsmouth as the most powerful hitter of a ball I have come across and for craft I put Len Shackleton of Sunderland on top of the list. Shackleton would always try something like a screw shot or a swerve shot. He could be relied upon to be unorthodox. It was certainly no good expecting a straightforward shot from 'Shack'. You never knew just what he intended to do.

Throughout his playing days there were many memorable games for Gil. The following story was remembered by both the men involved:
Gordon Astall recalls: 'I enjoyed playing with Gil, although as a winger I was well away from his area of influence. That was until Gil was hurt because in those days of no substitutes I was the replacement 'keeper!

The only reason I was the replacement 'keeper was because I'm a bloody sports idiot, you ask me to do something related to any sport and I'd do it.

Fortunately Gil wasn't injured very often and I can only recall two occasions when I was called up; against Spurs and Chelsea. We got well and truly hammered by Spurs and they had a penalty! It was either White or Smith who took it and the first time they approached the ball they stopped just to make me even more nervous.'

Gil remembers: 'It was 31 August 1957, we were playing Chelsea at Stamford Bridge in front of a crowd of 43,806. I went up for a ball and as I came down Jimmy Greaves was going up and he caught me under the jaw. I was carried off and ended up with seven stitches. Dick Neal went into goal. At half-time I was lying on a bed nursing my injury when Ticker came in and threw the goalkeeper's jersey at me in disgust, saying, "That's the last time I'm doing that!" We were losing 5–0. Gordon Astall went in and we eventually lost 5–1 with Eddie Brown scoring.'

In recalling his playing days Gil fondly remembers the camaraderie among the Blues players, 'As a young footballer I could not have had a better group of players to grow up with, every day in the dressing room was a laugh, it was like being at the Birmingham Hippodrome!'

It seems that Gill also had an impact on the younger players when he was older, too.

As John Newman recalls: 'I was a young upcoming player while Gil was the established senior professional. I always looked upon him as being Birmingham City Football Club. When I went to a reunion a few years ago, for which Gil had given his apologies, a shadow was cast over the whole event because he is such an integral part of the club. He's Mr Birmingham City!

He was never short of giving advice to younger players and was particularly helpful to me regarding my FA Cup Final appearance in 1956, although regrettably the whole occasion passed me by.

The spirit in that team was great and we were very successful: Division Two Champions, FA Cup runners-up and FA Cup semi-finalists in the three years between 1955–57.

I remember sitting beside Gil on the way back from Middlesbrough, who we had beaten by either four or five goals to one. We had started to talk about promotion to Division One and I asked him did he think we were good enough. His reply was typical Gil: "We're a better side than we've ever been since we've been together."'

George Edwards recalls: 'I played two games as an amateur for Swansea City as a 17-year-old before World War Two started. The war not only meant that my football career stalled but also my academic studies, as I wanted to be a teacher. There was always this link between Gil and I with the impact of the war on our careers and the education connection.

I was playing for Coventry City where Harry Storer was the manager. When Harry moved to Blues he asked me to go with him to "join a big club in

Birmingham". I said I would as long as he could get me a place at Birmingham University to continue with my MA, which he did.

The only thing I knew about Birmingham City was Gil Merrick, as he was already a well-known footballer. St Andrew's was in a terrible state; no stands, no cover at all, just terraces – you had to climb over an embankment to get to the pitch.

I was with Blues from 1945–49 and we were an extremely effective defensive unit built on the dependability of Gil. We won the Football League South in 1945–46 (Villa were second!) and only conceded 45 goals. One of the players, Cyril Trigg I think, had a betting scheme going whereby if the opposition scored he paid out £1 and if they didn't he got £1, that season he made a profit of £10, which was a lot of money in those days!

Gil was a very prominent member of the team – he was so safe and reliable. He was a nice chap and sociable but you had to get to know him. I think I half got to know half of him!

He was never flash, unlike some of his contemporaries, Sam Bartram for example. On one occasion I remember Sam Bartram taking a penalty at St Andrew's and his cannonball shot crashed against the crossbar and rocketed into the air to land on top of the net. Sam had to stampede back to prevent us scoring.'

While spending time with Gil in preparing his biography I became impressed by his modesty, on occasions I literally had to 'drag' from him facts related to his incredible life in football and to his time at Birmingham City Football Club. There were no scrapbooks of his career, no cupboards and drawers full of memorabilia, just a few selected photographs to remind the visitor they were in the home of one of Britain's greatest sportsmen of the 1950s.

Gil played in goal for Birmingham City over 720 times, including some 170 appearances during World War Two. His senior appearance record of

551 games is unlikely to be surpassed as players today do not stay with clubs long enough to challenge such records.

During his 551 senior appearances he conceded 666 goals which represents a game average of 1.21 per game. Bearing in mind that a goalkeeper is the last line of defence and that there are five other defenders contributing to clean sheets, it is worth noting that Gil's biggest goals against for Birmingham came late on in his career when Preston North End beat Blues 8–0 at Deepdale on 1 February 1958. Prior to that he was beaten seven times by Tottenham Hotspur in the 7–1 defeat on 18 September 1957 at White Hart Lane. Two 6–0 defeats were endured on 10 December 1955 by Bolton Wanderers at Burnden Park and on 3 September 1958 by West Bromwich Albion at St Andrew's.

At 38 years of age Gil was the oldest player to play first-team football for the Blues during the 22 years he spent as a player, and he made 145 consecutive appearances between 1949 and 1952. He kept 20 clean sheets from 36 appearances in 1947–48, a record which was only beaten in 1997–98 by Ian Bennett, who kept 21 clean sheets.

Five goals went past Gil on nine occasions, five of which happened during season 1957–58:

Season	Date	Opposition	Venue	Score
1951–52	19 April	Notts County	Away	5–0
1952–53	29 November	Notts Forest	Home	5–0
1953–54	6 February	Fulham	Away	5–2
1956–57	13 April	Tottenham Hotspur	Away	5–1
1957–58	31 August	Chelsea	Away	5–1
1957–58	28 September	Sheffield Wednesday	Away	5–3
1957–58	12 October	Wolverhampton Wanderers	Away	5–1
1957–58	26 December	West Bromwich Albion	Home	5–3
1957–58	22 February	Wolverhampton Wanderers	Away	5–1

In the 533 League and FA Cup games in which Gil performed between the sticks Blues won 231 games, drew 133 and lost 169. Season by season detail is displayed below:

Season	Played	Won	Drew	Lost
1946–47	45	27	5	13
1947–48	36	19	13	4
1948–49	43	11	15	17
1949–50	43	7	14	22
1950–51	48	24	10	14
1951–52	43	21	9	13
1952–53	42	20	12	10
1953–54	40	17	9	14
1954–55	31	18	5	8
1955–56	44	22	9	13
1956–57	47	18	11	18
1957–58	29	8	13	8
1958–59	40	18	8	14
1959–60	2	1	0	1
Total	533	231	133	169

CHAPTER FOUR
England

I t took me eight years to get international recognition. I played my first representative game at Wembley at the age of 21. Having established myself in the Blues first team, I was picked to play for the Civil Defence against the Combined Services.

It was an evening game watched by approximately 40,000, which was the biggest crowd I had played in front of at that stage. We lost by five goals. I could not have been that impressive as Ted Drake scored a hat-trick.

The teams were:

Civil Defence		*Combined Services*	
Merrick G.	(Birmingham)	Ditchburn E.	(Spurs)
Bicknell C.	(West Ham)	Male G.	(Arsenal)
Dawes F.W.	(Crystal Palace)	Ferrier H.	(Barnsley)
Owen W.M.	(Newport County)	White R.	(Spurs)
Affleck D.	(Southampton)	Oakes J.	(Charlton)
Magnall D.	(QPR)	Burgess R.	(Spurs)
Spence R.	(Chelsea)	Kurz F.	(Grimsby Town)
Dawes A.	(Crystal Palace)	Edelston M.	(Reading)
Foreman G.A.	(West Ham)	Drake E.	(Arsenal)
Goulden L.	(West Ham)	Tennant A.	(Chelsea)
Thorley E.	(Huddersfield)	Smith L.	(Brentford)

For the next two seasons I played for the FA, twice against the RAF at Coventry and once against Combined Services at Portsmouth – I was on honeymoon when I read of my selection for the game.

Ted Ditchburn and Bert Williams were my opposition in those three games, and the three of us challenged for the top honour in the years that followed. I eventually took Williams's place in the England side, with Ditchburn as my goalkeeping colleague, in 1953.

There was a match for the APTC (Army Physical Training Corps) against the FA at Wembley. Frank Swift, the original choice, had to stand down and was replaced by Reg Allen of QPR. This move brought a protest from a brigadier who demanded that an APTC man should play, which was reported in the *Daily Express* as follows: 'This is a tough break for Allen and a lucky one for Merrick who could edge the gigantic Swift out of the England team by giving a really tip-top display. He is certainly destined to play for England soon.' That was in May 1946.

In October 1947 I made my debut for the Football League, which was generally regarded as one of the main stepping stones to getting full international selection. The game was against the Irish League at Windsor Park, Belfast.

Football League: Merrick, Woodruff (Burnley), Robinson (Middlesbrough), Taylor (Liverpool), Brown (Burnley), Emptage (Manchester City), Matthews (Blackpool), Pye (Wolves), Stubbins (Liverpool), Hagan (Sheffield United), Langton (Blackburn).

We won 5–3 and I was not happy about conceding those goals. Soon after the start I had made a clearance from my hands when the centre-forward blocked the ball and at the same time played it into the net. That was hardly an impressive start!

I had a break of 18 months before my second chance came in May 1949 when I was 27. The League of Ireland provided the opposition in Dublin and we won by five clear goals, which meant the selectors saw little of me in a one-sided game.

England were due to play Ireland on 16 November and Bert Williams was known to be unfit for the game so I was very hopeful of being selected, but the talk was that Bernard Streten of Luton Town was in the frame. As he had not played in any Inter-League matches I was hugely disappointed, thinking my chances had gone!

I played against the Irish twice in 1950 but the following season it was back with Williams and Ditchburn, plus the new name, Allen of Manchester United, pushed me out of the Inter-League scene.

So that was it until 1951–52, when Allen was selected for the first Inter-League game of the season against the League of Ireland at Goodison Park, which they won 9–1. It may have been that lone goal that was indirectly responsible for me getting my cap. Allen had nothing to do in the game except on one occasion, and then he let the ball trickle through his hands into the net; it was the price of inactivity. Three weeks later the Football League was due to play the Scottish League at Hillsborough on a Wednesday afternoon and everyone expected Williams to be back in goal. On the Monday night I was sitting in our treatment room at St Andrew's, having some work done on a minor injury, when Bob Brocklebank came in and said, 'Williams is injured and can't play at Sheffield; they want you up there right away to take his place.'

This was it – a real chance in a big game. I took my opportunity, making more saves in the match than all my other Inter-League games put together. It was nearing the end and we were winning 2–1 when I saved a penalty from Willie Waddell to win us the game. Ironically, five days earlier at Bramall Lane, Sheffield, I made a very similar save from Alf Ringstead.

I will remember it as my most successful game, with perhaps my most successful moment also coming in the match – that save from Waddell's penalty. That, in fact, ensured a Football League victory, to make it all the more pleasing. The great winger ran at a slight angle towards my left, and because he came at the ball obviously meaning to hit it hard I had a clue about the direction the ball would take. A player shaping to hit a penalty hard and in one particular direction cannot successfully change his mind at the last second. That is why the man who takes two paces to the ball and can place it accurately to either corner without 'showing out' is the most dangerous penalty taker a goalkeeper can face. Waddell cracked the ball midway between me and the post and about waist height. I just had time to meet the ball with my left fist and it seared away over the bar. A glorious moment to remember!

A fortnight after that penalty save the Football League side from that afternoon was chosen for the full international against Northern Ireland. The news that gave me my most wonderful individual moment came as I was at school taking a PT class. A local Birmingham newspaper phoned through to say that I had been selected to play for England against Ireland on 14 November 1951 and in my own home town at Villa Park. Twelve years after signing as a professional I had reached the top!

Walter Winterbottom, the England manager at the time, had played as an amateur for Manchester United at centre-half before World War Two. An educated man, he joined the Football Association as a result of his wartime army service, becoming director of coaching prior to managing the England side. He would often ask players to play in different positions to those they did for their club; for example, Billy Wright played inside-right against Austria to specifically mark Ocwirk.

Walter was a nice bloke but an amateur who let the players get on with it. He did not understand man management, which was evidenced when we had been knocked out of the World Cup in 1954. The squad were relaxing in the hotel grounds one afternoon when he came over to us and announced in front of everyone that Billy Wright and Jimmy Dickinson would be staying over to watch the Final match. The rest of us were effectively told we were not wanted, which was an enormous blow to team morale.

Gil's England matches

1. v Northern Ireland at Villa Park, 14 November 1951   Won 2–0

England: Merrick, Ramsey, L. Smith, Wright, Barrass, Dickinson, Finney, Sewell, Lofthouse, Phillips, Medley.

The selectors experimented by giving inside-forwards Jackie Sewell and Len Phillips their first caps either side of Nat Lofthouse, who scored a goal in each half. Birmingham City goalkeeper Gil Merrick made the short journey to Villa Park for his first of 23 caps. He kept a clean sheet, but was lucky in the second half when a screaming 25-yard shot from Barnsley forward Eddie McMorran crashed against the crossbar. Skipper Billy Wright gave a vintage performance. He was the boss both of the defence and the midfield. His tackles were panther-like in their speed, and then he always found a teammate with a well-judged pass.

2. v Austria at Wembley, 28 November 1951   Drew 2–2

England: Merrick, Ramsey, Eckerseley, Wright, J. Froggatt, Dickinson, Milton, Broadis, Lofthouse, Bailey, Medley.

An injury to Tom Finney forced yet another permutation by the selectors, with Gloucester cricketer and Arsenal forward Arthur Milton partnering Ivor Broadis on the right wing. Austria, under the baton of the remarkable Ernst 'Clockwork' Ocwirk, took the lead in the 47th minute after a first half of cut and thrust football of the highest quality. Ocwirk sent a precision free-kick into the penalty area where Melchior forced it wide of goalkeeper Gil Merrick. England equalised in the 70th minute when the ice-cool Alf Ramsey scored from the penalty spot after his Spurs teammate Eddie Baily had been sent sprawling. Six minutes later Ramsey made a goal for Nat Lofthouse with a pinpointed free-kick, which the Bolton centre-forward steered high into the net with a powerful header. Austria, rated one of the best sides in Europe and fresh from becoming the first overseas team to beat Scotland at home, saved the match two minutes from the end with a penalty by Stojaspal. There were some breathtaking attacking movements by both teams, yet all the goals came from set-piece play. Milton was the last player capped by England at cricket and football. When Eddie Baily was fouled for the penalty, he picked himself up and said to his Spurs teammate Alf Ramsey, 'I've done all the hard work winning the blankety blank penalty, now make sure you score.' Alf tucked the penalty away as coolly as if in a training session.

3. v Scotland at Hampden Park, 5 April 1952   Won 2–1

England: Merrick, Ramsey, Garrett, Wright, J. Froggatt, Dickinson, Finney, Broadis, Lofthouse, Pearson, Rowley.

Two neatly taken goals by Stan Pearson stretched England's unbeaten run in full internationals at Hampden Park to 15 years. His first after eight minutes was a superb hooked shot, and his second just before half-time followed a mix-up in Scotland's defence. The Scots screamed that they were robbed of a penalty when Gil Merrick pulled down Lawrie Reilly, and the 134,504 crowd roared with rage when the referee waved play on. Reilly managed to score in the last minute, Scotland's first home goal against England since the war. But it was too late to stop an England victory that gave them a share of the Home Championship with Wales. Blackpool's Tom Garrett made a sound debut at left-back in place of the injured Bill Eckersley.

4. v Italy in Florence, 18 May 1952   Drew 1–1

England: Merrick, Ramsey, Garrett, Wright, J. Froggatt, Dickinson, Finney, Broadis, Lofthouse, Pearson, Elliott.

Only Billy Wright and Tom Finney remained from the England team that had conquered Italy 4–0 in Turin in 1948. Ivor Broadis gave England a fourth-minute lead that was cancelled out by a spectacular solo effort from Amadei in the 63rd minute. The idolised centre-forward Piola, who had helped Italy retain the World Cup in 1938, was recalled for a swansong appearance at the age of 39. It ended on a sad note for him when he missed an easy chance for a winner in front of an empty net. It was the cool heads of Wright and Ramsey that brought England safely through to a draw when the Italians were threatening to run riot in the second half.

Gil recalls: The English players were on their way from the dressing rooms to go out and meet Italy in the first match of our tour. We were in a 60 yard long, gloomy tunnel that ran under part of the playing arena, and way ahead of us was a patch of light where the tunnel opened out into the stadium directly behind the goal. When we came up through that tunnel-exit the greatest roar I have ever heard nearly turned my stomach over with excitement. The crowd, waving white jockey caps, yelled and yelled over and again, working up to one mad crescendo – 'Italia!' But that wasn't all. As we lined up for the presentation, the biggest throng of photographers I have ever seen in one place – there must have been a hundred of them – crowded round our line taking pictures from every conceivable angle.

5. v Austria in Vienna, 25 May 1952   Won 3–2

Team: Merrick, Ramsey, Eckersley, Wright, J. Froggatt, Dickinson, Finney, Sewell, Lofthouse, Baily, Elliott.

This was the match that earned Nat Lofthouse the nickname 'The Lion of Vienna'. Eight minutes from the end, with the game deadlocked at 2–2, Tom Finney collected a long throw from Gil Merrick and released a pass that sent Lofty clear just inside the Austrian half. He galloped 45 yards with a pack of defenders snapping at his heels, and collided with oncoming goalkeeper Musil as he released a shot. He was flat out unconscious and did not see the ball roll over the goalline for the winning goal. The Bolton hero was carried off on a stretcher, but, still dazed, returned for the final five minutes. He struck a shot against a post in the closing moments. England's counter-attacking tactics had worked to perfection. They had taken the lead in the 21st minute after soaking up non-stop pressure from the Austrians, who were rated the number-one team in Europe. A penetrating pass by Eddie Baily opened the heart of the Austrian defence and Lofthouse finished off the move with a left-foot volley deep into the net. The cheers of the squads of British soldiers in the 65,500 crowd were still filling the Prater Stadium when Jack Froggatt conceded a penalty from which Huber side-footed an equaliser. The Portsmouth centre-half quickly made amends with a pass that put Jackie Sewell through to score after he had wrong-footed the Austrian defenders with two exaggerated dummies. Austria pulled level again just before half-time through centre-forward Diego, who shrugged off Billy Wright's challenge before powering the ball past goalkeeper Gil Merrick. Then came the storybook climax from Lofthouse. The triumphant England players were carried back to their dressing room on the shoulders of cheering Tommies, who had come from their posts in Germany in their thousands.

Gil recalls: It was 1952 and Austria were perceived as being the Champions of Europe. This was in the days before the European Championship began, and their captain had been crowned European Footballer of the Year. Both England and Austria were unbeaten that season, having held us to a draw some months before at Wembley; therefore, the match in Vienna was looked upon as being the match to decide who was the best international side in Europe. The crowd was swelled by the attendance of over 1,000 British servicemen who were given leave to attend the game. The atmosphere was fantastic. It was 2–2 with about six minutes to go when the Austrians won a corner on the right. I managed to catch the ball and cradle it to my chest. As I did that Dienst, the Austrian centre-forward, slapped the ball hard with his hand in an attempt to get me to drop the ball. I held on but the referee did not see it. I turned away from the ruck of players, bounced the ball once and quickly took a view of the field. There was Nat Lofthouse and Tom Finney within two or three yards of each other near the centre circle. I hurled the ball 35 yards up to Finney, who crossed the ball first time to Nat Lofthouse. Nat ran 40 yards to score the winner and from that day was known as 'The Lion of Vienna'. The Tommies went mad! I often wonder what would have happened if I hadn't been able to hold onto that ball and it had been knocked out of my hands. They would probably have scored and history would have been very different.

6. v Switzerland in Zurich, 28 May 1952   Won 3–0

England: Merrick, Ramsey, Eckersley, Wright, J. Froggatt, Dickinson, R. Allen, Sewell, Lofthouse, Baily, Finney.

Billy Wright was credited with taking over the England caps record from Bob Crompton with this 43rd international appearance (although most record books give Crompton's old record as 41 caps). The Swiss were beaten by the same scoring combination that had won the match in Vienna three days earlier: Jackie Sewell scored one, Nat Lofthouse two. West Bromwich Albion's versatile forward Ronnie Allen won the first of his five caps, and gave a lively performance on the right wing.

7. v Northern Ireland at Windsor Park, 4 October 1952   Drew 2–2

England: Merrick, Ramsey, Eckersley, Wright, J. Froggatt, Dickinson, Finney, Sewell, Lofthouse, Baily, Elliott.

Nat Lofthouse scored in the first minute and Billy Elliott in the last minute of a dramatic match. Sandwiched in between was the magic of Celtic ball artist Charlie Tully, who scored twice for Ireland. He beat Merrick from 25 yards and then again with his specialist inswinging corner-kick after the Irish team had been reduced to 10 men by injury. (In a game for Celtic, against Falkirk, Tully netted directly from a corner and was ordered to retake it because the referee was not ready. He immediately repeated the trick and put the ball in the exact same spot in the net!) Northern Ireland, urged on by a record 60,000 Windsor Park crowd, had two young midfield partners called Danny Blanchflower and Jimmy McIlroy dictating the pace and the pattern of the match. They were on the verge of their first victory over England since 1927 when Elliott silenced the celebrating fans with an equalising header in the desperate closing moments. Billy Wright and Jimmy Dickinson were the match stars for England, steadying the ship with their cool defensive work when the Irish threatened to take a stranglehold on the game. Team manager Walter Winterbottom was furious over the goal that Charlie Tully scored direct from a corner-kick. Charlie was famous for his inswinging corners, and England had worked at cutting them out in training by placing Alf Ramsey on the near post and then centre-half Jack Froggatt directly behind goalkeeper Gil Merrick. The corner from which he scored was curling towards Ramsey, who suddenly ducked under the ball. Gil reached out but only caught thin air as the ball swung into the net. Alf said later that he thought Gil had shouted 'mine', but it had apparently been one of the Irish forwards. The crowd went berserk when the ball hit the net. And no wonder – it was Northern Ireland's first international goal for 18 months!

8. v Wales at Wembley, 12 November 1952   Won 5–2

England: Merrick, Ramsey, L. Smith, Wright, J. Froggatt, Dickinson, Finney, R. Froggatt, Lofthouse, Bentley, Elliott.

This was the first time Wales had ever played at Wembley, and a Wednesday afternoon crowd of 93,500 paid record gate receipts of £43,000. England were two goals up in the first 10 minutes through Tom Finney and Nat Lofthouse. Five minutes later Trevor Ford pulled a goal back for Wales, and was then involved in a collision with Jack Froggatt that led to the England centre-half being carried off. Billy Wright switched to the middle of the defence, with Billy Elliott dropping back from the wing to left-half. Jack Froggatt, whose cousin, Redfern, was making his debut at inside-right, came back on as a passenger on the left wing. Remarkably, it was Jack who scored England's third goal just before half-time with a brave diving header. Roy Bentley made it 4–1 in England's first attack after half-time, with Ford instantly replying for Wales. Nat Lofthouse rounded off the scoring with a shot from 25 yards that goalkeeper Bill Shortt could only help into the net. The significant thing about this match was that it was the first time Billy Wright played at centre-half for England.

9. v Belgium at Wembley, 26 November 1952   Won 5–0

England: Merrick, Ramsey, L. Smith, Wright, J. Froggatt, Dickinson, Finney, Bentley, Lofthouse, R. Froggatt, Elliott.

Nat Lofthouse kept up his one-man bombardment with a double strike that took his haul to nine goals in five games. Redfern Froggatt scored his first goal for England, and Burnley winger Billy Elliott netted twice against the outplayed Belgians. The game was played in a driving sleet, with ice patches forming on the famous Wembley turf making it difficult for defenders to keep their feet. England led 2–0 at the end of a first half in which they might have had half a dozen goals against a completely outplayed Belgian team.

10. v Scotland at Wembley, 18 April 1953   Drew 2–2

England: Merrick, Ramsey, L. Smith, Wright, Barrass, Dickinson, Finney, Broadis, Lofthouse, R. Froggatt, J. Froggatt.

Lawrie 'Last Minute' Reilly equalised for Scotland with the final kick of the match. It was Reilly's second goal in reply to two from Ivor Broadis. The Scots, driven from midfield by Preston's Tommy Docherty and Dundee's Doug Cowie, dominated play for long spells and thoroughly deserved their late equaliser. They played for much of the second half with only 10 men after Rangers left-back Sammy Cox had been injured trying to stop a thrusting run by Tom Finney. Utility player Jack Froggatt, capped by England at centre-half and as an outside-left, partnered his cousin Redfern on the left wing. Each of the cousins missed simple chances to give England the lead before Broadis scored what looked like being a winning second goal. This draw meant that it was 19 years since England had last beaten them on home ground. There were just 30 seconds left when Lawrie Reilly popped up with one of his typical late goals that so often saved Scotland.

11. v Argentina in Buenos Aires, 17 May 1953   Abandoned 0–0

(Abandoned at 0–0 after 23 minutes following a rainstorm)

England: Merrick, Ramsey, Eckersley, Wright, Johnston, Dickinson, Finney, Broadis, Lofthouse, T. Taylor, Berry.

The pitch became waterlogged following a cloudburst and British referee Arthur Ellis, up to his ankles in water, had no alternative but to abandon the game. Three days earlier an Argentinean XI had beaten an FA XI 3–1 in an unofficial international watched by a crowd of 120,000, including Juan Peron and his wife, Eva. The selectors had to wait to see if the new left-wing partnership of Manchester United teammates Tommy Taylor and Johnny Berry would work at international level. Referee Arthur Ellis, later to make a name for himself in television's *It's A Knockout*, was quite a joker. As he signalled for the teams to return to the dressing rooms, he said to Billy Wright, 'If we stay out any longer we'll need lifeboats!' The pitch just disappeared under a lake of water, and England's kit was so wet that the players needed help from the training staff to strip off.

Gil recalls: It was the day we played Argentina in the storm of Buenos Aires. After being presented to President Peron we went down the one end for the pre-match warm up. I put my dad's old cap and a second pair of gloves in the corner of the net as usual, and then individual photographs were wanted. After about five minutes of this, I happened to go back into the net to fetch a ball out. The second pair of gloves were there but the cap had gone. I never thought I would feel so bad over losing a bit of old rag!

Running around the pitch and our goal was a crowd of scruffy little youngsters, and one of them must have whipped the cap as a souvenir. I often wondered what the lad said to himself when he unwrapped the bundle and had a really good look at it.

12. v Chile in Santiago, 24 May 1953   Won 2–1

England: Merrick, Ramsey, Eckersley, Wright, Johnston, Dickinson, Finney, Broadis, Lofthouse, T. Taylor, Berry.

Tommy Taylor's first goal for England in the 48th minute was a freak. His intended cross was turned into the net by Chilean goalkeeper Livingstone-Eves, who was the son of a Scot. Nat Lofthouse scored the second decisive goal after one of a dozen, thrusting runs by Finney, and three minutes later he headed another Finney cross against the bar. The Chileans scored their only goal seven minutes from the end when a Rojas shot was deflected wide of the diving Gil Merrick.

13. v Uruguay in Montevideo, 31 May 1953   Lost 2–1

England: Merrick, Ramsey, Eckersley, Wright, Johnston, Dickinson, Finney, Broadis, Lofthouse, T. Taylor, Berry.

World champions Uruguay turned on an exhibition against the old masters and might have trebled their score but for being over elaborate with dazzling approach play. Abbadie gave Uruguay the lead in the 27th minute and centre-forward Miguez made it 2–0 on the hour. Nat Lofthouse and Ivor Broadis struck the woodwork and Tommy Taylor scored in the closing moments after an Alf Ramsey shot had been blocked. It was a spirited fight back by England after they had struggled to hold the world champions in a one-sided first half. Miguez, a master of ball control and as crafty as a monkey, led the entire England defence a merry dance. Billy Wright, winning his 50th cap, played him as well as any defender could do, but several times he was left tackling his shadow.

14. v Wales at Ninian Park, 10 October 1953   Won 4–1

England: Merrick, Garrett, Eckersley, Wright, Johnston, Dickinson, Finney, Quixall, Lofthouse, Wilshaw, Mullen.

Dennis Wilshaw celebrated his first England cap with two goals, and Nat Lofthouse netted twice for the second successive match. All of England's goals came in the 10 minutes either side of the half-time interval after Wales had taken a deserved 23rd minute lead through Ivor Allchurch. Wales played for much of the game with left-back Alf Sherwood as a passenger on the wing after he had been concussed in the 32nd minute. Giant Leeds centre-forward John Charles might have had a hat-trick but for a succession of superb saves by England goalkeeper Gil Merrick. Albert Quixall, literally worth his weight in gold when sold by Sheffield Wednesday to Manchester United for £45,000 in 1958, made his England debut at inside-right at the age of 20. Wales were unlucky not to have salvaged a draw from a game they often dominated. As in 1949–50, the Home Championship was used to determine Great Britain's qualifiers for the World Cup finals. There were more than 60,000 fans packed into Ninian Park, and the atmosphere was similar to when the Welsh stoke up for their rugby internationals. England were hugely flattered with the size of the victory. This was the beginning of the rise of the greatest Welsh football team in their history, with John Charles and Ivor Allchurch laying the foundations for their memorable careers.

There has never been a more gifted all-round British footballer than Big John. He was equally effective at centre-forward or centre-half, and once he had moved to Juventus from Leeds he developed into the perfect player. He not only had great technique, but also the ideal temperament. His nickname 'the Gentle Giant' was misleading because he could be as physical as Nat Lofthouse one minute and then as beautifully balanced as Tom Finney the next. He was commanding in the air and could head with the force of Tommy Lawton. When the conversation gets around to who has been the greatest British footballer of all time, John tends to get left out of the argument because he spent so much time in Italy, but he should be in anybody's top six players.

15 v Rest of World at Wembley, 21 October 1953   Drew 4–4

England: Merrick, Ramsey, Eckersley, Wright, Ufton, Dickinson, Matthews, Mortensen, Lofthouse, Quixall, Mullen.

Rest of World: Zeman (Spain), Navarro (Spain), Hanappi (Austria), Cajkovski (Yugoslavia), Posipal (West Germany), Ocwirk (Austria), Boniperti (Italy), Kubala (Spain), Nordahl (Sweden), Vukas (Yugoslavia), Zebec (Yugoslavia).

An Alf Ramsey penalty in the last minute gave England a draw in a showpiece match to mark the Football Association's 90th birthday. England trailed three times against the European all-stars in a Wednesday afternoon match that provided a feast of football for the 97,000 spectators. Forty-six years later FIFA saw fit to downgrade the game to non-international status, but the Football Association awarded Billy Wright a cap and it stays in English records as a full international. That was good news for talented Charlton defender Derek Ufton, a solid batsman and understudy at Kent to wicketkeeper Godfrey Evans, who won his only cap in the game. England took the game very seriously because there was a lot of pride and prestige at stake. Considering they had only been together for a couple of days, the Rest of Europe side played some magnificent football. The pick of the players was Ladislav Kubala, who had been the first of the outstanding Hungarians to switch his football allegiance to Spain. Ask anybody from Barcelona or Budapest and they will tell you that he was in the class of Puskas. He had wonderful ball control and the ability to make space for himself with clever changes of pace. A naturally gifted genius, Kubala left Hungary just before the rise of their greatest of all teams. Just imagine how good they would have been had he still been available for selection! Kubala AND Puskas to mark. The mind boggles! The scorers in the game were Mullen with two, Mortensen and Ramsey with a penalty.

In an article entitled, 'Talking it over' in *Charles Buchan's Football Monthly* for December 1953, John Thompson reported, '...but already gaps are showing in the English defence. Too much is left to Gilbert Merrick. This fine goalkeeper is to give one of his most splendid displays.'

Charles Buchan in his regular column 'In My Opinion' said, 'With the international tournament well on its way, it is disturbing that the FA selectors are no nearer finding a settled England team than they were when the season started...It seems that the only positions on which their minds are made up are goal and wing-half, where Gil Merrick, Billy Wright and Jimmy Dickinson hold undisputed sway.'

It is worth noting that in the 23 internationals played by Gil, the only two players who played in all of those 23 matches were Billy Wright and Jimmy Dickinson.

It would seem that Charles Buchan was proved right because of the 41 players that played with Gil in his 23 appearances only five gained 10 caps or more.

Player	Games	Player	Games
Alf Ramsey	15	Tommy Taylor	5
Lionel Smith	4	John Berry	3
Malcolm Barrass	2	Albert Quixall	3
Tom Finney	20	Dennis Wilshaw	3
Jackie Sewell	6	Jimmy Mullen	6
Nat Lofthouse	18	Derek Ufton	1
Les Phillips	1	Stanley Matthews	5
Les Medley	2	Stan Rickaby	1
Bill Eckersley	11	Harold Hassall	1
Jack Froggatt	9	Ernie Taylor	1
Arthur Milton	1	Stan Mortensen	2
Ivor Broadis	13	George Robb	1
Eddie Bailey	4	Ron Staniforth	6
Tommy Garrett	3	Roger Byrne	6
Stan Pearson	2	Harry Clarke	1
Jack Rowley	1	Johnny Nicholls	2
Billy Elliott	5	Sid Owen	3
Ronnie Allen	3	Peter Harris	1
Redfern Froggatt	3	Bedford Jezzard	1
Roy Bentley	2	Bill McGarry	2
Harry Johnston	6		

16. v Northern Ireland at Goodison Park, 11 November 1953   Won 3–1

England: Merrick, Rickaby, Eckersley, Wright, Johnston, Dickinson, Matthews, Quixall, Lofthouse, Hassall, Mullen.

Harold Hassall, playing alongside his Bolton teammate Nat Lofthouse, scored the first of his two goals in just 30 seconds to mark his international recall after two years. It was Hassall's fifth and last cap. Eddie McMorran equalised for the Irish nine minutes after half-time, and they were the superior side for long periods. Stanley Matthews turned the game England's way with a typical mazy run on the hour before passing to Billy Wright, who set up a simple second goal for Hassall. It was Nat Lofthouse who wrapped up victory for England 15 minutes later when he headed in a Jimmy Mullen cross, colliding with goalkeeper Smyth as he powered the ball into the net. Lofthouse limped off and Smyth was carried off with a broken nose. West Bromwich right-back Stan Rickaby played in his one and only England match in place of the injured Alf Ramsey.

17. v Scotland at Hampden Park, 3 April 1954   Won 4–2

England: Merrick, Staniforth, R. Byrne, Wright, H. Clarke, Dickinson, Finney, Broadis, R. Allen, Nicholls, Mullen.

The England selectors made eight changes to the team taken apart by Hungary. Johnny Nicholls had good reason to remember his debut. It was his 23rd birthday and he celebrated with England's second goal, a flying header from a Tom Finney cross. Playing alongside his West Bromwich Albion teammate Ronnie Allen, he was one of four debutants, along with

Ron Staniforth, Harry Clarke and Manchester United left-back Roger Byrne, who was to prove himself one of the finest players ever to wear the number-three shirt. Clarke, a 31-year-old centre-half, followed Ditchburn, Ramsey, Willis, Nicholson and Medley as members of the Spurs 'push-and-run' team who were capped after the age of 30-plus. Roared on by a vast crowd of 134,554, Scotland took the lead in the seventh minute through Blackpool's Allan Brown. Ivor Broadis equalised eight minutes later after penetrating approach work by Wright and Finney. It was the same combination of Wright and Finney that set up England's second goal by birthday boy Nicholls five minutes into the second half. Headed goals by Allen and Jimmy Mullen wrapped the game up for England and guaranteed them going to the World Cup Finals as home champions. Scotland scored a strange second goal in the last minute when a cross from Willie Ormond suddenly swirled into the net.

See Chapter Five 'The Hungarians' for Gil's 18th game.

19. v Yugoslavia in Belgrade, 16 May 1954   Lost 1–0

England: Merrick, Staniforth, R. Byrne, Wright, Owen, Dickinson, Finney, Broadis, R. Allen, Nicholls, Mullen.

Syd Owen of Luton Town was the 11th centre-half tried since the defection of Neil Franklin to the outlawed Colombian league. England concentrated on a deep defence and a counter-attacking policy, and almost got away with a draw. Jimmy Mullen, Ronnie Allen and Johnny Nicholls had shots saved during breakaway raids, but the Yugoslavs were generally in control. They were always the sharper side and deserved their winning goal three minutes from the end when a 35-yard free-kick was deflected by Owen into the path of Mitic, who scored from six yards. This was Tom Finney's 50th international for England, and England wanted so much to get at least a draw to mark the occasion. Tom was arguably the finest player to wear the England shirt in the early post-war years. Stanley Matthews was the people's favourite, but most of the professionals would have given Tom the nod just ahead of Stanley because there was so much to his game. He was comfortable in any forward position, could dribble almost as well as Stanley and was as brave as a lion. The defeat in Yugoslavia did little to help confidence levels as England went on to Budapest for the return match.

20. (See Chapter Five 'The Hungarians') World Cup 1954 Switzerland

Whatever the World Cup in Switzerland may have lacked in atmosphere following the carnival across in Brazil in 1950, it more than made up for on the pitch by producing, statistically, the most entertaining tournament of all-time. In all, an incredible 140 goals were scored in 26 matches, at a mind-boggling average of over five per game. Chief goal-grabbers were Hungary – a team brimming with talent, invention and skill and the undisputed favourites to make their label as the 'best team in the world' official.

Hungary came into the tournament boasting an unbeaten record that stretched back more than four years, with the likes of Kocsis, Bozsic and Hidegkuti being the key figures. However, it was their captain and spiritual fulcrum, Ferenc Puskas, that epitomised their brilliant pioneering style of play. Just months before the World Cup, Hungary had humbled and humiliated England 6–3 at Wembley and 7–1 in the return in Budapest.

Gil had first-hand experience of the side dubbed 'The Magnificent Magyars' in those two matches as well as in Switzerland.

Gil recalls: The preparation was nothing like it is now, no initial squad of 40 reduced to a travelling squad of 22. Fifteen players travelled, and don't forget there were no substitutes in those days. My understudy was Alan Hodgkinson of Sheffield United. We got to the fourth round after playing Belgium twice and Switzerland and faced Uruguay in a temperature of well over 100 degrees Fahrenheit. It was incredibly hot and of course we were in our winter shirts. That was my last game for England after being replaced by Bert Williams of Wolves.'

21. v Belgium in Basle, 17 June 1954   Drew 4–4 after extra-time

England: Merrick, Staniforth, R. Byrne, Wright, Owen, Dickinson, Matthews, Broadis, Lofthouse, T. Taylor, Finney.

A Jimmy Dickinson own-goal during extra-time gave Belgium a draw in a helter-skelter match full of defensive blunders as England made an eventful start to their challenge for the World Cup. A goal down in five minutes, England produced some enterprising and energetic football and deserved their 2–1 half-time lead from goals by Ivor Broadis and Nat Lofthouse. The Lofthouse goal was a cracker, a spectacular diving header to send a Tom Finney cross powering into the net. When Broadis added a third goal early in the second half it looked almost certain to be an England victory. Then defensive lapses let the Belgians in for two soft goals that took the game into extra-time. Nat Lofthouse made it 4–3 in the opening moments of extra-time, and England seemed destined for full points when Jimmy Dickinson turned an intended headed clearance into his own net. Billy Wright took over at centre-half in the closing stages as Syd Owen limped to a passenger's role on the wing. It was to prove the most significant positional switch of Billy's career.

22. v Switzerland in Berne, 20 June 1954   Won 2–0

England: Merrick, Staniforth, R. Byrne, McGarry, Wright, Dickinson, Finney, Broadis, T. Taylor, Wilshaw, Mullen.

Wolves left-wing partners Dennis Wilshaw and Jimmy Mullen scored the goals, and their club captain Billy Wright started his first match as England's centre-half. Bill McGarry gave a solid debut performance in Wright's old position at right-half against the host nation and in searing-hot conditions that sapped the energy of the players. Mullen scored the first goal three minutes before half-time to silence a capacity crowd of 60,000. Wilshaw clinched the victory with a superb individual goal midway through the second half, cleverly evading three Swiss defenders before steering a firm shot into the net. Syd Owen's injury had accidentally solved England's on-going centre-half crisis. Billy Wright slotted into the position as naturally as if born to the job, and the Swiss centre-forward was not allowed a sniff at goal.

23. v Uruguay in Basle, 26 June 1954   Lost 4–2

England: Merrick, Staniforth, R. Byrne, McGarry, Wright, Dickinson, Matthews, Broadis, Lofthouse, Wilshaw, Finney.

Two mistakes by goalkeeper Gil Merrick let defending world champions Uruguay in for goals that turned this quarter-final match in their favour after Nat Lofthouse and Tom Finney had each scored to give England hope of causing an upset. Shuffling Stanley Matthews, the undisputed man of the match, hit a post and had a shot pushed off target before Uruguay clinched victory with their fourth goal in the 84th minute when Merrick failed to save a speculative shot from Ambrois. It was a shell-shocked Merrick's final match for England. He had let in 30 goals in his last 10 games after conceding only 15 in his first 13 internationals. The Uruguayans had beaten Scotland 7–0 in a qualifying round match, but were never allowed to show that sort of superiority by an England team that performed with pride and purpose.

Gil recalls: Playing for England was a tremendous honour, particularly when you consider the competition I had to beat off for the goalkeeper's jersey.

That first cap was very special and there was only one place it was going and that was to my dad. He was extremely proud of it but unfortunately it got mislaid over the years. I have never been one for hoarding memorabilia or keeping scrapbooks, but I would love to have that first cap in my possession. The others were given to my son and daughter, Birmingham City had one, I gave one to the Birmingham City Historical Society and there might be a few around the house, but I can't account for all 23.

My most prized piece of memorabilia was the yellow jersey I wore for England when we beat Austria 3–2 in Vienna. Normally you had to return all the kit to the English FA, but all the players were so elated after that victory that we asked Walter Winterbottom if we could keep our shirts and he agreed. I never wore it but kept it in my kit bag, then, over time, I lost track of where it was. Then 15 years ago I was in hospital in Solihull for a hip replacement (I've had three) and one of the nurses told me that she had my England jersey. It transpired that she was the daughter of Ray Devey, who was a trainer at Blues, and she had it after Ray's death. I was a bit disappointed as I never gave it to Ray so how he got hold of it I will never know. I couldn't ask for it back could I?

Being an international footballer meant I got to see the world and this was before travelling to foreign countries was considered to be a normal activity. The Football Association's tour of America in 1953 was an incredible education. It was the most ambitious tour covering over 23,000 miles.

They came in their thousands to greet us at the airport in Buenos Aires. It was an hour or more before we finally got away after speeches, photographs and interviews. It was bewildering. When we went for a meal a hundred people would gather to stare at us through the window. They preferred photographs to autographs, everyone seemed to have a camera.

Argentina in 1953 was something like England in the 21st century, their players were rewarded well financially. A good player would earn £120 a month and at the end of the season received a bonus of a month's money. Ten per cent went to the player when he was transferred. Many additional payments were available, with advertising providing the main source. A goalkeeper could collect £125 from a firm if he saved a penalty.

Colonel Peron offered to raffle a Mercedes car among the squad if they beat England in their two games – one was abandoned but as they won the other he kept his word and one of the players drove off in a brand new car!

Tom Finney recalled in his book The Autobiography: *'Merrick became the scapegoat for our elimination from the tournament. I felt desperately sorry for him. He was criticised unmercifully in the media. England's public enemy number one according to them. They slaughtered him for days and seemed to have ganged up to ensure that he was banished from the international arena forever. If that was the aim, it worked; Gil never again pulled on the England jersey. All players make mistakes and no one individual should ever carry all the responsibility for a result, irrespective of how poorly he might have played. Goalkeepers always suffer for a bad game because their mistakes are vital. If I get a second life, remind me not to come back as one!'*

CHAPTER FIVE
——————— *The Hungarians* ———————

England: Merrick, Ramsey 1 (pen), Eckersley, Wright, Johnston, Dickinson, Matthews, E. Taylor, Mortensen 1, Sewell 1, Robb.

Hungary: Gyula Grosics (goalkeeper), Jeno Buzánszky (right-back), Mihály Lantos (left-back), József Bozsik (right-half), Gyula Lóránt (centre-half), József Zakariás (left-half), László Budai (right-wing), Sándor Kocsis (inside-right), Nándor Hidegkuti (centre-forward), Ferenc Puskás (inside-left), Zoltán Czibor (outside-left), Gusztáv Sebes (manager).

This was England's first defeat by foreign opponents on home territory, and it is the match that changed the face of English football. The Hungarians, Olympic champions and on a run of 29 successive matches without defeat, played to a flexible 4–2–4 formation and made England's 2–3–5 pattern seem about as outdated as a hansom cab on a motorway. Nandor Hidegkuti, a deep-lying centre-forward, nipped in for a hat-trick as two-goal Ferenc Puskas pulled the defence inside out. England were flattered by the 6–3 scoreline. Alf Ramsey, Bill Eckersley, Harry Johnston, Ernie Taylor, Stan Mortensen and George Robb never played for England again, with Taylor and Robb making their debuts. Hungary had given just a taste of what was to come in the first minute when Hidegkuti collected a through ball from Puskas, deceived centre-half Johnston with a distracting dummy and then fired the ball high into the net from 20 yards. Gil Merrick was left flapping in mid-air. Moments after Sewell had equalised in the 15th minute, England were flattened by a 13-minute burst of Magyar magic. Two goals from the purist Puskas and another from the elusive Hidegkuti made it England 1, Hungary 4. The 100,000 Wembley spectators could not believe their eyes. Stan Mortensen pulled it back to 4–2 by half-time. However, any hope England had of getting back into the game died within 10 minutes of the second half. First the cultured Jozef Bozsik scored with a rising drive and then Hidegkuti completed his hurricane hat-trick when he put the finishing touch to a dazzling succession of passes that ripped the England defence apart. Alf Ramsey scored a late penalty after his Tottenham teammate George Robb, a schoolmaster, was pulled down by goalkeeper Grosics. The final scoreline could easily have read 10–3 to the Hungarians. Billy Wright had never been given such a chasing in all his life as the one he got from Ferenc Puskas.

Budapest, 23 May 1954   England lost 7–1

England: Merrick, Staniforth, R. Byrne, Wright, Owen, Dickinson, P. Harris, Sewell, Jezzard, Broadis 1, Finney.

This was the biggest defeat in England's 90-year football history (and continues to be so to this day). Just four of the England team from the 6–3 slaughter at Wembley in November had survived: Merrick, Wright, Dickinson and Finney. Fulham centre-forward Bedford Jezzard made a best-forgotten debut, while the unfortunate Peter Harris was winning his second and last cap after a gap of five years. His first cap had come in the 2–0 home defeat by the Republic of Ireland in 1949. The Hungarians, leading 3–0 at half-time, were six goals clear and cantering before Ivor Broadis opened the scoring for England. Hungary immediately replied with their seventh goal scored by Puskas from a pass by Hidegkuti. Hungary's scorers were Puskas (2), Kocsis (2), Lantos, Toth and Hidegkuti. Billy Wright came off with his face as white as his shirt and looking like a man who had seen a ghost come back to haunt him. As hard as this giant-hearted man tried, he could not get near to suppressing the irrepressible Puskas.

Gil remembers: It was an incredibly hot May day and in those days we knew nothing about nutrition and none of us had taken on enough liquids. Poor old Syd Owen became so dehydrated that he went as rigid as a board and we had to carry him off.

The man who kept goal for England when they were famously beaten by Ferenc Puskas's Hungary 53 years ago paid tribute to his old opponent and said: 'It was a privilege to be done by them.'

Gil Merrick, now 84, remembers the occasion as if it was yesterday and is mourning the passing of Puskas.

England had never been beaten by an overseas side at Wembley until Hungary arrived and triumphed 6–3, and Merrick could not stop the floodgates opening, although he went on to pay tribute to his opponent.

It was a day to remember for everyone when we faced Hungary. Their football was far in advance of ours. They were just too good for us. I could only do my best which I did.

Puskas, in his book, said that if I hadn't had a good game they would have had 12. Well that's how I looked at it!

It was [a] privilege to play against Hungary even though we got done. We had not played against a foreign side like that.

You had to appreciate the Hungary team. They were a great side and brought a different kind of football to England. During the first half of the match the football played by the Hungarians was a style never seen before; their passing, running, dribbling was amazing and all done at pace with accuracy. At half-time the players had to try and sort it out as the management had little knowledge of tactics! We only lost the second half 1–2, but for the whole game we were under pressure, it was like being at The Alamo. That was the day the game changed, Hungary had set the standard even to the extent that they played in a lightweight kit. The nearest I've seen to the way the Hungarians played that day was the Arsenal Premiership winners of 2003–04.

A few years ago a TV company were planning a film on Puskas and they wanted to use Wembley as the location. The three surviving members of the England squad, myself, Jackie Sewell and George Robb, were requested to be involved. We agreed but the TV company couldn't raise the funding and the project fell through.

Gil says of the Hungarian star: Not only was Puskas a great footballer, but he was a lovely man. He had not been well for a number of years and I wrote to him in hospital. It is a sad day for football.'

Merrick was considered one of the best 'keepers of his day, but became known as 'Mister Thirteen' after the number of goals he conceded in the two matches against Hungary.

As we walked off 4–2 down at half-time at Wembley our centre-half, Harry Johnson, turned to me and said, 'Gil, I haven't had a kick! I don't know who to mark!'

CHAPTER SIX
─────── *The FA Cup Final – 1956* ───────

Final v Manchester City at Wembley, May 1956   **Lost 3–1**

Blues: Merrick, Hall, Green, Newman, Smith, Boyd, Astall, Kinsey, Brown, Murohy, Govan.

Manchester City: Trautmann, Leivers, Little, Barnes, Ewing, Paul, Johnstone, Hayes, Revie, Dyson, Clarke.

Scorer: Kinsey
Attendance: 100,000
Referee: Mr A. Bond (Middlesex)

The one-armed man blew his whistle and tears rolled down the cheeks of one nine-year-old boy – the author. It was impossible – the eight-inch Marconi black and white television (the only TV at our end of the street) must be mistaken – Kenneth Wolstenholme had just declared that Manchester City had won the FA Cup, beating Birmingham City by three goals to one! Thank goodness there were no pundits, slow motion replays and endless analysis, as it would have been too much to bear.

It was 4.45pm on a sweltering May afternoon and the hottest favourites ever to win the coveted trophy had been well and truly beaten. How could it have happened?

Birmingham City had got to Wembley without playing a game at home, beating the mighty Arsenal, Sunderland and West Bromwich Albion on the way. It had all started in January with a 7–1 demolition of

Torquay United and a 4–0 humiliation of Leyton Orient – they had scored 18 goals and only conceded two.

Mr Bond, the referee for the Final, was also the referee on 7 January when Blues began their Cup run with a victory away at Torquay. The Torquay goal is described in the following account:

'Torquay supporters were treated to a goal of their own to cheer, albeit a freak one by their best player, Shaw. He chased what seemed a lost cause with the ball wide on the right rolling out of play; however, he caught it and crossed it in one movement from right on the byline which Gil seemed to gather cleanly from under the cross bar. After an appeal from the Torquay players the referee awarded the goal, not even consulting his linesman, who must have had a better view of whether or not the 'keeper had landed over the line while holding the ball.'

The team had five full internationals: Jeff Hall, Trevor Smith, Gordon Astall and Gil for England, and Noel Kinsey for Wales. Eddie Brown and Peter Murphy were scoring goals for fun, amassing 44 League and Cup goals before the fateful day. Birmingham City had finished sixth in Division One of the Football League – their highest finish in the top division to date (this is still true in 2009).

The blue side of Birmingham were in despair while the claret and blue supporters could not resist a wry smile. The Blues had lost their fighting spirit: an early goal, the battle in the Wembley cauldron and, most importantly, they had lost the chance of a major trophy. However, the tale began well before the match...

Such was the confidence in the city that one of the sports newspapers known locally as *The Blue Mail* ran a 'mock-up' photograph of Len Boyd the captain on the shoulders of the Blues players holding the FA Cup aloft.

At the time no one considered this to be tempting fate, it was simply a prediction of the inevitable outcome of a future event.

Manchester City had been the losing finalists the year before, missing out to Newcastle United 3–1. Eight of their 1956 team were still in the current squad and had already experienced the phenomenon of playing at Wembley. In the Birmingham side, only Gil had played there before when on England international duty.

On Saturday evening commemorative banquets had been held for the players of Manchester City and Birmingham City in two London nightspots no more than a stone's throw apart.

The day had seemed so promising, with the teams coming out to a huge roar from the 100,000 fans crammed into the ground. The 5 May was a lovely hot day, but not ideal for 90 minutes of English football.

The teams had had to change from playing in their normal colours: the Blues chose white shirts with black facings, black shorts and black socks with a white turnover, while Manchester plumped for a claret shirt with thin white stripes, white shorts and hooped socks that matched their shirts.

After the introduction to the Queen, the game kicked-off, and everything seemed perfect – until the third minute. Revie, starting the move 10 yards from his penalty area, swung over a long pass which cleared the head of Hall. Clarke raced in from behind to deliver a return ball to Revie who had made ground quickly. The ball was back-heeled square to Hayes inside the area, and he hit a crisp first-time shot past Merrick. Even then this was viewed as a stimulant – something to get Blues quickly into top gear.

Unfortunately it did not, and although Blues hit back with a Kinsey shot which went in off the post to equalise 11 minutes later, there was still something lacking in their overall performance. Their spirit, prominent in other rounds, simply was not there when it was needed the most. When the Blues' famous battle cry 'Keep Right On' failed to raise the tempo after the goal, things began to look ominous. Blues held on until half-time with the scores remaining level, but they were clearly frustrated by the astute offside trap employed by Revie's men. Manchester City started off the better team in the second half, and were 2–1 up after 65 minutes. Johnstone, running at Green on the right, was presented with an opportunity to feed Dyson, who had run diagonally across the field to the edge of the area. A perfectly timed pass allowed Dyson to take the ball in his stride and fire past Merrick as he came out to narrow the angle. The winning team then put the game well beyond Blues' reach with a sucker-punch goal three minutes later. It came from a Blues attack: Trautmann dived bravely at the feet of Brown, took the ball from him and kicked long upfield. It was flicked on by Hayes into the path of Johnstone, who had sprinted clear of the static defence. He finished with a lovely strike into the bottom corner. Moments later Trautmann received treatment after a collision with Murphy while saving Brown's header at goal. The goalkeeper played on for 20 minutes, despite holding his head in agony. Any shot on target would have made a save impossible in his condition, but Blues failed to trouble him further. The game and the Blues FA Cup dream withered for another year.

The Stan Halsey report in the Sunday Pictorial *on 6 May. Oh, what a wonderful Manchester double. United carried off the League Championship and now City have deservedly run off with the Cup.*

Some people called Manchester City the team of 'old crocks' because of their many injured men. Those folk must be wearing a rather lopsided smile this morning.

Not until 11 o'clock on the morning of the match did Manchester manager Les McDowall finally select his team. All week the Manchester camp had been alive with rumours of injuries. Then Spurdle developed a painful boil under the arm and McDowall's team problem was solved. Revie came in to the centre and Johnstone played outside-right.

Bill Leivers, right-back, and Bobby Johnstone both had a shot of Novocaine just before the game to dull the pain in injured legs.

Roy Clarke, left-winger, played with a displaced bone in his right leg. At one point in the game it came out of joint again and he had to pause in his play and put it back himself!

It was Don Revie's experience of Wembley last year that came to Manchester's aid yesterday. He realised that to rush about all over the place is not good on the Wembley turf. So Manchester used the open spaces. They made Birmingham chase them and in trying to do so they chased themselves out of the Cup.

At the end, the Kinsey–Brown–Murphy inside-forward trio looked the most forlorn footballers on the field. They were completely done.

Manchester City took the lead in three minutes. A master move brought the goal. Leivers sent the ball to Revie who crossed it to Clarke. Then Revie called for a quick return square pass, stepped over the ball and, hey presto, there was Hayes to hit it into the net.

Birmingham was badly jolted by that early shock.

Centre-half Smith steadied them up, however, and in the 15th minute Kinsey and Brown engaged in a duet which baffled the Manchester defence and Kinsey scored the equaliser.

The heartening effect of that goal inspired Birmingham to their best spell in the game. They reached a standard of football that indicated they might yet beat Manchester.

But Manchester's tactics gradually brought them the ascendancy. And that brief bit of Birmingham spirit flickered out.

Dyson, with his tendency to dally where direct action is needed, was the player everyone expected would be the big flop of the forward line.

But in the twentieth second-half minute with the score 1–1, and both teams sweating and fidgeting after the vital lead goal which might so easily mean victory, it was Jack Dyson who rose to the crisis – and scored.

A little earlier he tried a snapshot that Birmingham back Jeff Hall cleared from the line. Then came a brilliant pass from Revie – one of the many sparkling football touches with which he celebrated his return to Wembley.

Dyson did not fail. His shot went true to the net.

Three minutes later Dyson the scorer became Dyson the goal maker. This time he steadied a long ball, stabbed it accurately over to Bobby Johnstone, emergency right-winger, who sent Birmingham sagging into the depths of Cup despair with a coolly taken goal.

The last fifteen minutes were rough and tough for goalkeeper Bert Trautmann. He ricked his [neck] when coping with a tackle by Murphy and was shaken again when he collided with Ewing, his own centre-half. It was Ewing's tactics of following the centre-forward to the wings while the backs and half-backs covered the front of the goal gap he left.

This completely broke the effectiveness of Birmingham's Eddie Brown.

After the match, Cup-winning captain Roy Paul, the froth of celebration champagne still on his lips, said, 'We'll have another go at the Cup next year. Expect us back at Wembley.'

Paul agreed that Manchester City had dictated the pace of the play with a purpose: 'It was the result of our experience last year, when we ran ourselves to death with 10 men.

It's no good running with the ball at Wembley. It takes too much out of you. So if the pace looked a bit slow – that's the reason. We wanted it that way.'

Jack Peart – Sunday Pictorial – commented: …and what wide-open spaces there were! Birmingham's covering was shocking and they played without fight or bite except for the 15 minutes after their equaliser. The only star in defence was centre-half Trevor Smith. He had a thankless task trying to cover all the gaps in a defence as leaky as a colander. I didn't blame Gil Merrick for any of the goals but I thought Jeff Hall, England's right-back against Brazil next Wednesday, had a nightmare of a game. Skipper Len Boyd looked like a fish out of water at left-half. Far better to have taken a chance with Jack Badham there and kept Boyd on his favourite right flank.

This reference to Len Boyd being played out of position was due to an injury to the usual occupant of the number-six shirt, Roy Warhurst, who was hurt in the sixth-round victory over Arsenal on 3 March at Highbury. Up until then Warhurst had played every League and Cup game in a very settled side, which with a few occasional changes due to injury had been: Merrick, Hall, Green, Boyd, Smith, Warhurst, Astall, Kinsey, Brown, Murphy and Govan.

Boyd missed four League games in December 1955 and had been replaced by the dependable John Watts and the Blues claimed a single win. When Warhurst missed a game in October 1955 his shirt went to Peter Warmington, who made only two appearances all season, the second being the last League game prior to the Wembley Final when he replaced Peter Murphy, with the number-six spot going to Albert Linnecor.

A number of reserves were used to try and replace Warhurst during the months of March and April 1956: Linnecor, Badham, Watts and, for the match against Sunderland at Roker Park on 18 April, Boyd played at right-half with Johnny Newman playing at the number-six spot. Prior to this experiment Newman had played 12 games, 11 of which were at centre-half deputising for Trevor Smith.

The speculation as to who would replace Warhurst was rife and Eric Woodward wrote on the subject in *The Blue Mail* before the big game in an article entitled 'Who gets the job? Everybody knows except Arthur Turner'.

Anyone for Wembley? The biggest puzzle outside the Kremlin at the moment is the composition of Birmingham City's team on the Great Day next week. And it will not be solved until much nearer zero hour, probably next Friday when Blues are tucked away in their pre-final training quarters.

You can name most of the team and be right. But who is the lucky person to take over from the unfortunate Roy Warhurst? Cast a glance down the talented second string line up at St Andrew's and you will see there's not much in it.

Johnny Newman, Jack Badham, Albert Linnecor…they must all stand a chance of selection and they have the necessary qualifications. Bill Finney, Johnny Watts…the list could go on.

But I am not going to risk criticism and profoundly tell you this is it; this will be the 11 manager Arthur Turner will put out to bring the Cup back to St Andrew's, because honestly, I don't know what it will be – and neither does anyone else at the moment. As Mr Turner pointedly remarked to me during the week: 'Everybody knows what it will be – except me.'

Let's get this straight. The Blues chief is not being deliberately shy. He is carefully sifting the pros and cons of his final decision. Now he must know what the American pilot who dropped the first A-bomb felt like. For it is, indeed, quite a decision to make.

The plain fact is that manager Arthur Turner has confidence in each and every one of his second-string men, but he has to be doubly confident this time. And the decision rests upon him, and him alone.

This week Blues held a secret, behind-closed-doors practice game between first team and reserves. 'It's to keep the edge on the lads and get them used to white shirts,' explained Mr Turner.

No doubt he also took the chance to run the rule once more over the candidates for the wing-half vacancy and see how the team as a whole shapes up for the big game. Mr Turner's sole objective at the moment is to turn out the side which, in his opinion, will stand the greatest chance of lifting the Cup.

That's why there will be at least one more very private practice match next week before the lads move off to Twyford on Thursday afternoon.

And remember, Blues will be training right up to Friday lunchtime. They do not move off to their hide-out until after a training session on Thursday afternoon. They train again on Friday morning at the Huntley & Palmers ground. And they'll have a look at Wembley's magic turf on Friday afternoon.

For the superstitious-minded, I remind them that Blues' away-from-it-all headquarters are the same used by Albion's Cup-winning side two years ago.

By the time the Birmingham City party are touring the stadium I expect the side will be chosen and announced.

And you can take it from me that the men on the fringe of selection have much to think about.

Johnny Newman, for instance. He bears the 'best reserve centre-half in the country' label quite calmly and with infinite modesty. Fact is Johnny would rather be an ordinary first team player than a great reserve.

Fact also is that with any other team but Blues he would be able to be just that. But Blues found him, fostered him and moulded his game. It's just a trick of fate that he should have to act as stand-in to a player who is a ripe old 20 years of age. Johnny accepts this with calmness.

But he must surely be inwardly excited at the prospect of a place in the Wembley sun.

Then there's Jack Badham. He would rather be away like a rocket than have publicity about himself – but the fact remains that he is the greatest club-man in the game today. Full-back, half-back or forward – it all seems the same to Jack.

He gives all he's got all the time. And he's never failed yet. Last season he served up some wonderful stuff on the last stretch towards promotion, after being plucked from the shadow of the reserve side and put into the limelight. A great tactical move from Mr Turner worked to a 'T'.

Then this season Warhurst was injured and the menace of Charlie 'Cannonball' Fleming had to be curbed in the semi-final. 'Send for Jack' was the cry – and Badham did it again. How can he, too, be possibly out of the running?

There's nothing wrong with Albert Linnecor – except lack of experience. Yet cheery Albert, an 'unknown' to most before he was brought up from the reserves to play at Huddersfield, has had a fantastic rise to the big-time.

His debut was on 7 March – just nine games ago. And he has played in only four first-team games all told. Yet in that time his polish and precision have automatically put him in the running for a Wembley place. Amazing isn't it and it just goes to show what a player Albert is going to be with more experience.

Bill Finney? He has played a dozen first-team games since arriving from Stoke City – yet he's only been on the losing side once! Finney doesn't wear lucky charms around his neck. He is another obvious contender.

My sympathies go out to manager Turner for the not-so-pleasant job on his desk. But being the honest man he is, no doubt the Blues manager will be glad to be in a position to sit and choose for such a great occasion.

Remember this…for the one who is chosen, someone has to be left out. And whoever they are, spare a thought for the effort and endeavour they, too, have put in to such a memorable season.

The Daily Mirror *on Monday 7 May 1956 by Bill Holden: 'Skipper Boyd Wins Medal For Courage'. Now it can be told…the inspiring story of the courage and determination of Len Boyd, Birmingham's left-half and captain, who went through two weeks of torture to win a Cup finalist's medal.*

For two weeks before the Final Len was encased in a plaster cast.

It was his one chance of getting fit enough to play…And the cast was taken off only one hour before the match began.

On April 19, with the final sixteen days away, a specialist discovered that

Boyd was developing a slipped disc. This caused a pressure on his spinal nerves and produced intense pain.

The only way to correct the trouble and remove the pain was for Boyd's body to be held rigid in a cast. From then on Len slept, trained and actually played in practice games while wearing the cast.

'It was uncomfortable, and Dave Fairhurst, our physiotherapist, regularly added strong adhesive bandage to it to make sure it kept in place,' Len said.

'When it was finally taken off we discovered it was ten pounds in weight. Often it felt heavier when I began to sweat while training, but it was more than worth it. I was able to play and never once felt a twinge of pain during the match. Some people thought I might still be suffering from fibrositis. I wasn't. I never have. But we thought it best to let everyone go on thinking it was that.'

Only Boyd's wife, Doreen, Birmingham City officials and *Mirror Sport* knew just how close Len came to having to take a seat on the sidelines. 'That fight for fitness was as tense as any encounter on the field, and we pledged to keep it secret until Len had collected his finalist's medal.'

Gil remembers: We'd played Manchester City in the 1955 FA Cup competition in round six. It was 12 March at St Andrew's and there were 58,000 fans in the ground. They won 1–0 thanks to a deflected Roy Clarke free-kick which hit me on the right wrist and my head before entering the net in the 88th minute. Roy Warhurst described it as 'the biggest fluke in football I ever saw.'

Many of the Manchester City side that ultimately played in the FA Cup Final of 1955 were in the 1956 team, the only absences being Jimmy Meadows (replaced by Leivers), Bill Spurdle (replaced by Dyson) and Fagan (replaced by Clarke). This experience was to prove vital in defeating Blues.

Prior to the Final in May 1956, Charles Buchan covered the game in his Opinion column under the title 'I Take Birmingham For The Cup'. Birmingham City are favourites for winning the FA Cup at Wembley. I have no doubt they will have the backing of most of the public, for one reason – they have never won the Cup.

It is strange how soccer followers have a soft spot for teams who have never previously won major competitions. They like to see the honours go round.

It is Birmingham's second final at Wembley. The first was in 1931, when they were unlucky, I thought, to be beaten by West Bromwich Albion, who won promotion from the Second Division, as well as the Cup, that year.

A controversial decision by the referee played a big part in the game.

Midway in the first half, Gregg, the Birmingham inside-left, headed a goal that, from my position high up in the Press Box, looked a very good one. Referee A. Kingscott disallowed it as offside.

It came from a free-kick taken by Cringan, Birmingham right-half, from a position near the half-way line.

When Cringan took the kick, it appeared to me that Gregg was onside. He ran forward and headed the ball into the net, only to find that the referee had blown his whistle.

A goal at that stage would probably have put Birmingham on the winning track.

As it turned out, Albion went ahead through a goal scored by 'Ginger' Richardson, Albion centre-forward.

Though inside-left Bradford equalised in the second half, Birmingham never fully recovered. Richardson scored the winning goal late in the game.

Bradford's goal was the first equaliser to be scored in a Wembley Final. Yet up to the last minute it was doubtful whether Bradford would play. He had a pulled thigh muscle.

Though he scored with a wonderful 25-yard shot, Bradford, I thought, was unfit for such an important game. And of course it caused a big controversy in Birmingham.

As you know Birmingham have reached this year's Final without playing a home tie at St Andrew's.

They have defeated Torquay United (7–1), Leyton Orient (4–0), West Bromwich Albion (1–0), Arsenal (3–1) and Sunderland (3–0); a goal average of 18–2.

I expect them to cap it all with a resounding triumph against Manchester City, provided they get over the first 15 minutes of Wembley 'nerves'.

Apart from goalkeeper Merrick, playing at the classic stadium will be a new experience for them. But their teamwork is so polished that I believe they will soon settle down in the tense atmosphere.

Manchester City – or at least eight players – were in the Final last May. They were beaten 3–1 by Newcastle United after struggling gallantly for an hour without right-back Jimmy Meadows who badly injured his right knee. They should not be overawed by the occasion.

This is the second time Manchester City have appeared at Wembley in successive seasons. The first time was in 1933 and 1934.

On being presented with his runners-up medal after being beaten 3–0 by Everton in 1933, Manchester City captain and centre-half Sam Cowan said to Her Majesty the Queen: 'Never mind we'll be back again next year'. Prophetic words! City won their way to Wembley again the next May and beat Portsmouth 2–1.

This time they were helped by an injury to Portsmouth's tall centre-half Jimmy Allen, later transferred to Aston Villa for the record fee of £10,775.

There was only 15 minutes to play with Portsmouth leading 1–0 when Allen retired behind the goal with an injured knee. While he had treatment from the trainer, Fred Tilson, City centre-forward, equalised.

Though Allen returned shortly afterwards, City were on top and in the closing minutes Tilson scored the winning goal.

So Tilson, now on the City training staff, carried out a half-time boast. In the dressing-rooms, defenders had been bemoaning the goal they thought they should have prevented.

Tilson interrupted them. 'Stop worrying. I'll score a couple of goals in the second half to make up for it,' he said. He kept his word and City won the Cup for the second time.

The occasion proved too much for their 19-year-old goalkeeper. As soon as the final whistle sounded he fell flat on the ground in a faint. His name is Frank Swift.

Swift, who only twelve months earlier had watched the Final from the terraces behind one of the goals, became the best England goalkeeper for many years.

City's first Cup success came in 1904 when a goal by the great Welsh international outside-right, Billy Meredith, beat Bolton Wanderers. But the Wanderers had their revenge in 1926 when they beat City by the same score, 1–0. It was an unfortunate season for City. Besides being beaten in the Cup Final they were relegated from the First to the Second Division.

They had a chance to escape on the very last day of the season. They were at Middlesbrough and victory would have saved them. Unhappily for City, their outside-right, Austin, missed a penalty-kick and they went down. It is to be hoped that Manchester City will be spared the handicap of injuries this year.

Remember in addition to Meadows, they were deprived before last year's match of inside-forward Johnny Hart and outside-left Roy Clarke.

Manchester City's attractive style, built around the deep-lying centre-forward, Bobby Johnstone, the Scottish international, depends mainly upon first-class teamwork.

An injury to a key player can throw a spanner in the works. They will need all their attacking powers against such a strong defence as that of Birmingham, whose half-backs Len Boyd, Trevor Smith (a future England star) and Roy Warhurst have blighted the hopes of many teams.

At full strength, Manchester City are a delight to watch. Birmingham, too, are an attractive team so the Final prospects are pleasing. It should be a great game if the injury bogey does not raise its head.

Three of the last four Finals were marred by accidents to players. Bolton were hit by the injury to left-half Eric Bell against Blackpool. Arsenal had to fight for an hour against Newcastle United without left-back Walley Barnes. Last season, City lost Meadows after half an hour in the clash with Newcastle.

There can be no doubt that these injuries were the deciding factors. I trust there will be none this time.

An article in the Daily Mirror *by Peter Wilson on 7 May: 'I Shan't Forget The Merrick Touch'. It wasn't a Cup Final that tattooed itself into your memory – not as a contest anyway. For the winners were so superior for five-sixths of the game.*

Indeed, even at half-time, when the goals were shared, you would, had you been marking this like a boxing match, have made Manchester well ahead on points!

There was almost a foreign elegance about Manchester.

They were not quite so deadly as the Hungarians because their shooting was not so lethal.

But the impression you got was that they were able to perform at three-quarters speed – and still be a vital yard faster than these strangely clad 'lily-whites' who toiled and spun to such little purpose.

There can be no doubt as to the personality of the game – the enigmatic Pimpernel-like Don Revie.

In the past suggestions have been made that the Don of football is a trouble-maker. He certainly made trouble enough for Birmingham.

Birmingham centre-half Trevor Smith was like a man trying to pick up quicksilver with his bare hands.

And then Bobby Johnstone. There were times in the first half and even during the first ten minutes of the second when it looked as though he would never finish the match, so carefully was he 'favouring' his heavily bandaged left leg.

He finished the match – all right – for Birmingham – with that electric dash from a Trautmann clearance.

Trautmann too – what memories he recalled of the youth who was to grow into the goalkeeping giant called Swift. Twenty-two years ago 'Swiftie' collapsed at the final whistle the last time Manchester City won the Cup.

Trautmann reeling and weaving between the posts for the last quarter of an hour like a groggy fighter in his own corner, clasping his head as though to make sure it was still there, looked similarly on the point of no return.

And that was one little scene I shall not forget: beaten 'keeper Gil Merrick walking half the length of the field to support victorious but dazed Bert on his way to get his winner's medal.

But the incident I liked best was when Roy Little, having been laid low by a kick in the face from Gordon Astall, affectionately patted Astall on the head as soon as had regained his feet, to indicate that fault was at least partly his own. That's sportsmanship, my masters.

So final congratulations to the one-armed whistler, referee Alf Bond, who, despite one moment of indecision on a 'hands' verdict, had a good match. PREMIUM BOND YOU MIGHT SAY.

And here's to Birmingham. Even in their black hour there were no recriminations. Like everyone else, they admitted that the better team won.

The June 1956 edition of Charles Buchan's Football Monthly *match report: Manchester City, beaten in the final the previous season by Newcastle United, made handsome atonement by winning the FA Cup for the third time with a well-deserved clear cut victory over Birmingham. An early goal in the third minute by inside-right Hayes, inspired the Manchester men to one of the most impressive final victories ever achieved at Wembley. Birmingham plainly suffered from Wembley 'nerves' and the inability to adapt themselves to the spacious Wembley pitch. Centre-forward Revie, brought into the Manchester team at the last minute, revelled in the big occasion. His brilliant scheming and clever positioning was responsible for most of City's attacks. He had able support from Johnstone, Scottish international inside-forward, in the unaccustomed position of outside-right. It was a gamble by manager Les McDowall that came off.*

Johnstone's great skill led to City's second goal scored by Dyson in the 65th minute and he himself added the third goal four minutes later.

The Manchester defenders plainly profited from their Wembley experience of the previous season.

Ewing, an uncompromising centre-half, Paul, Leivers, the most polished full-back of the four, and Trautmann, despite an injury to his neck in the closing stages, were outstanding.

Birmingham were not the cast-iron team that had worthily built up a big reputation. They used up so much energy in stemming the lively Manchester men in the first half, they had no reserves to cope with more resourceful opposition in the second; a one-sided affair.

The only time Birmingham looked like pulling the game round was just after Kinsey equalised in the 15th minute. Then, until half-time, they were Manchester's equals. After the interval there was only one team in it.

John Thompson's monthly article, 'Talking it over' in the Charles Buchan's Football Monthly *of July 1956 provided a fitting footnote to this Wembley Final. For more years than I like to remember, I have studied the scenes in the Wembley dressing rooms when the teams have come from the field – the game won and lost.*

Among all those sad and happy memories I have never come across a team which has taken a triumph so calmly as did Manchester City. Nor have I known players so inconsolable as were Birmingham…Poor Birmingham! The grief of some of their players was understandable and I could sympathise with it. But as the players came through the tunnel from the field the [Birmingham] supporters gave them a great cheer and I saw their hero, Eddie Brown, wave to them and grin. And they cheered again.

The 1956 FA Cup Final team – where did they go?

Player	Outcome
Merrick	Retired 1960
Hall	Died 1959
Green	Retired 1959
Newman	Worcester City 1957
Smith	Walsall 1964
Boyd	Retired 1956
Astall	Torquay United 1961
Kinsey	Port Vale 1958
Brown	Leyton Orient 1959
Murphy	Retired 1961
Govan	Portsmouth 1958

Peter Murphy, in an interview with Peter Morris, discussed the 1956 Final in the February 1958 edition of Charles Buchan's Football Monthly *under an article entitled 'The Iron Men Were Crushed Because They Were Too Cocky', which read as follows:*

I have won a First Division championship medal with Tottenham Hotspur and a Second Division medal with Birmingham City, and I was delighted with

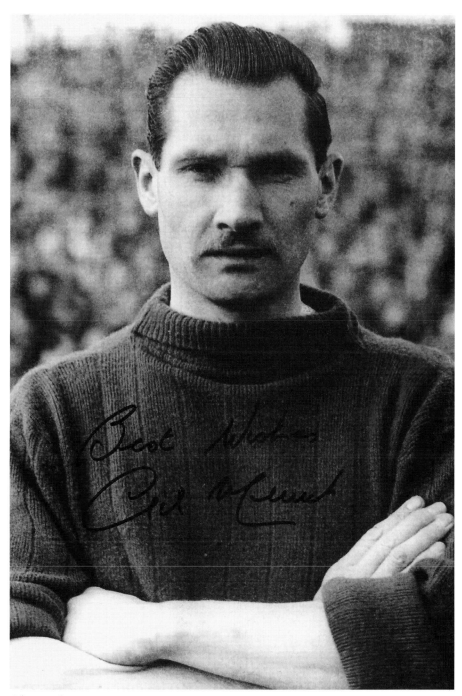

Gil Merrick.

October 1961: Gil on the pitch in Roma, trying to calm things down.

December 1941: Here we are boarding a Dakota at the Fleet Air Arm station near the Boot Inn at Honiley for our trip to play the BAOR (The British Army of the Rhine). It was a combination of players and officials, the players had to sit on the floor while the directors had bucket seats. Left to right: Neil Dougall, Turner, George Blackburn (trainer) W.A. Camkin (MD), Harry Dare, Gregory (secretary), Harry Morris (chairman), Jennings (sitting), Bodle, Mulraney, Massart, Harris, Edwards (sitting) and Storer. On the steps: Merrick, Dearson, Duckhouse and Len Morris (director).

Always number two – Peter Murphy is number three.

The 1956 FA Cup team line up. Gil was unavailable for the photo shoot so his head was superimposed onto Syd King's body.

Officials and players line up prior to a match against AIK Stockholm on the 1946 Swedish Tour. Players from left to right are: Arthur Turner, Gil Merrick, Ted Duckhouse, Frank Mitchell, Sid Owen (in tracksuit), Cyril Trigg, Fred Harris, Neil Dougall, Harold Bodle, Dennis Jennings, George Edwards and Jack Mulraney.

Boarding the train at New Street for summer training in Blackpool, c.1955. From left to right: Arthur Turner, Gordon Astall, Jeff Hall, Bryan Orritt, Albert Linnecor, John Watts, Gil Merrick, Trevor Smith and Alex Govan.

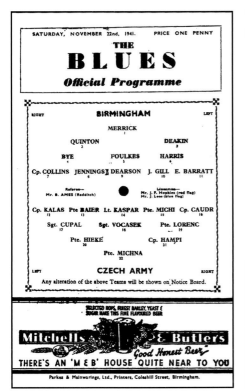

The programme for the match played on 22 November 1941. The score was 4–1.

Above right and below: The travelling alarm clock presented to players in the England v Rest of the World match to mark the 90th birthday of the FA, October 1953.

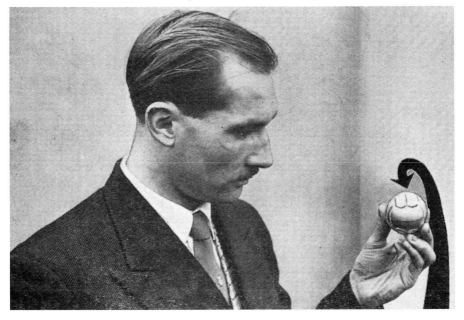

Bossing the goal area. Gil claims the ball from the Burnley centre-forward with Trevor Smith in attendance.

A goalmouth scramble with the ball evading Gil and Roy Warhurst.

Blues celebrate promotion to Division One at the end of 1954–55.

Celebrating promotion on the bench. Left to right: Dave Fairhurst, Arthur Turner, John Newman, Lack Lane, B. Bradbury and Gil Merrick.

League Cup winners, 1963.

The cover image on *I See it All*, 1954.

At Molineux, Gil Merrick thwarts Wolves centre-forward Jesse Pye following a left-wing centre. The other players in the picture are Dennis Jennings (behind Pye), Fred Harris (4) and Jimmy Dunn (8).

The 1956 FA Cup Final goalkeepers.

INTERNATIONAL SOCCER

EMPIRE STADIUM
VANCOUVER, B.C.

BIRMINGHAM CITY
(ENGLAND)

VERSUS

B. C. ALL-STARS

Saturday — June 10th, 1961
8:30 P.M.

PRICE 35¢ (33¢ + 2¢ TAX)

Gil smothers the ball at the feet of Joe Hayes in the 1956 FA Cup Final.

Gil dives to save, with T. Smith and H. Hooper onlookers.

Stan Lynn and Trevor Smith enjoy actually winning something!

Here I am talking to Bill Clinton's (the groundsman) assistant during pre-season about how long I wanted the grass on the pitch. Bill was a stickler for that and always delivered exactly what I wanted.

The team *c*.1943. Back row, left to right: S. Owen, T. Duckhouse, Gil, D. Massart, F. Harris. Front row: J. Mulraney, N. Dougall, D. Jennings, A. Turner, H. Bodle, G. Edwards.

On tour in Malmö, 1946. Back row, left to right: F. Harris, D. Dearson, A. Turner, Gil, F. Mitchell, D. Jennings, H. Storer (manager). Front row: J. Mulraney, N. Dougall, C. W. Jones, H. Bodle, G. Edwards.

Gil at his desk in the manager's office.

Gil on the terraces in 1961.

these honours, but even they cannot eradicate the disappointment I still feel whenever I think of Saturday May 5 1956.

That day Birmingham City, hottest FA Cup Final favourites since the War, crashed 3–1 to Manchester City. It ruined a St Andrew's Cup dream and that of Peter Murphy in particular.

They said we lost that final because we were too nervous. They said we had no answer to Don Revie. They said we played our worst football in the match that mattered most. They were wrong. WE LOST BECAUSE WE WERE TOO COCKY.

I say that now, some 18 months after that sunny but sad afternoon on the green Wembley turf.

Manchester City were the outsiders. They had been weakened by injuries before the game. A few weeks earlier we had taken a team which included five reserves to meet them in a League match at Maine Road. Although held to a 1–1 draw, we had outclassed them. No wonder we thought the Final would be a cake-walk.

It would be just a formality. The goals would come along in due course. There was nothing to worry about. No big match nerves in the dressing room before the game.

Well you know what happened. Manchester scored first – a delightful goal – and suddenly things were not going our way at all. Noel Kinsey put us level 15 minutes later, and I thought we were back in the game. But still things went wrong.

The fact was that gallant Manchester City were playing far better football than we thought they would. Inevitably, some of our players began to make mistakes.

Our tackling was nothing like so powerful as it had been in the previous rounds – all of which had been away from home except a replay against Carlisle. **(Author's Note: Wrong Peter!)**

I still think that had we not been tagged the 'Iron Men of Birmingham' we might have won.

I still believe our defenders were AFRAID to tackle in their usual manner because it was a Wembley Final and popular opinion would be against us if anyone got hurt. We were always at our best when our wing-halves were 'biting' in their tussles for midfield possession. It had been that way right from the third round.

Well someone did get injured and I was the Birmingham player involved in that disastrous collision with Bert Trautmann, late in the second half, when we were throwing in everything we had to force a goal.

Only Bert and I know just how close I came to scoring. Only I can tell of the fantastic dive which Trautmann launched to foil me.

I was so sure of netting in that instant that I was amazed when Trautmann flung himself at my feet from nowhere – I had been keeping half an eye on the Manchester City's centre-half, Dave Ewing.

If Bert had not been so quick off the mark I do not think he would have been hurt.

I was surprised when I heard how badly he had been injured. All I got was a bruise the size of a half-crown where his shoulder had thumped into my thigh. Had I scored then the game might have swung in our favour. But it was not to be, and so the most exciting Birmingham Cup run since 1931 crumbled to dust between the 66th and 69th minute when Manchester netted twice.

When Manchester United knocked us out in last year's semi-final at Hillsborough, I felt no real regret. We had done our best, but United were expected to win. But again the underdogs, in the shape of our old rivals and neighbours, Aston Villa, came up trumps and the FA Cup went to Birmingham after all – to Villa Park.

Once more I was firmly convinced that the best way to go on the field at Wembley is as rank outsiders. The slimmer the chance you are given, the surer – it seems to me – you are of winning. A funny game, football.

Which reminds me…how many clubs have won the championship of the Second Division and yet topped the table only once in the season?

That's what happened to Birmingham City when we won promotion in season 1954–55.

Our last game was at Doncaster, and we triumphed 5–1 to win the Second Division after spending the first half of the campaign in the bottom half of the table.

Doncaster must be my lucky ground, for it was there that I scored a hat-trick on my debut for Birmingham after being transferred from Spurs.

And it was my goal in April 1955 that proved the turning point of a vital game that had seldom looked like going our way. A strong wind and the hard ground did not suit our style of play and we thought we had done well to be drawing 1–1 at the interval. Then I made it 2–1 and we did not look back. We ran in three more goals against a demoralised Doncaster defence and promotion was ours at last.

All inside-forwards have their 'bogey men' and my two are those grand wing-halves, Bob Morton of Luton Town and Billy Nicholson of Spurs, now assistant manager at White Hart Lane. I have never had a good match against those two.

Gil's memories of the FA Cup Final

Pre-match Preparations

We travelled up to a small hotel outside Reading on the Wednesday prior to the match. On the following day we trained, a full session using the facilities of the local McVities biscuit factory.

On Friday we had a light training session to loosen up on the morning before travelling to The Grand Hotel at Paddington on the morning of the Final. We had a light lunch – I had fish – before leaving for Wembley an hour before kick-off.

In the period after lunch a few of us led by Len Boyd, who was a bit of comedian, went for a walk. Len decided to play a prank on Alex (Govan). We got to a public telephone box and phoned the hotel to speak to Alex. Len posed as a sports reporter for *The Sunday People* who wanted to do an article on how he felt immediately before the FA Cup Final. Alex had no reason to doubt the authenticity of the call and was pleased when the 'reporter' confirmed that a fee was payable. The rest of us were uncontrollable with laughter. When we got back to the hotel, Alex approached us to inform us of the fact that he was getting a fee for an article in *The Sunday People*. Len, keeping a straight face, said how lucky Alex was.

Sometime after the Final Len kept asking Alex if he had got the fee yet and if not he should chase it up. This went on for sometime until we were on a train and Len said to Alex, 'You see that guy sitting over there, he's the reporter from *The Sunday People*.' It wasn't until Alex threatened to go over and sort him out that Len confessed.

We were allocated the same dressing room as Blackpool used in 1953. I stayed in there and didn't go out onto the pitch prior to the game.

We stayed overnight in London with our wives to have a banquet that turned out to be something of a damp squib and which resulted in me making one of the biggest mistakes of my life, seriously diminishing our relationship.

John Camkin said he wanted me to meet someone at the nearby press club. I was reluctant to go but did in the end, leaving my wife on her own for over an hour, that was my big mistake. John introduced me to Alan Oaby who was a top reporter at the time and had slated me after my performance for England in the World Cup match against Uruguay, which we lost 4–2. Alan informed me that he had been told by David Wiseman to write a report that focused on the mistakes I had made. Because of

Oaby's reputation in Fleet Street, it was headline news. What I found out that night was that Wiseman had paid Oaby to write the article in that way!

Tickets

At the semi-final of the 1956 campaign, we were playing Sunderland at Hillsborough and winning 1–0 at half-time. As we came out for the second half, the Sunderland player Ted Purdon, who was ex-Blues and wasn't playing in the match, ran alongside me and touched me on the shoulder to say that Sunderland had been offered 200 Cup Final tickets per man if they won the game.

Len Shackleton played out of his skin that second half and for 20 minutes he ran the game. However, a second goal from Brown and a final one from Astall saw us through.

The ticket news was quite a talking point as the rule was 12 tickets each. A week or so later at our normal Thursday meeting it was suggested that as one of the senior players I should bring up the subject of Final tickets. The chairman Harry Morris was called to the meeting that was held in the players' room to be told that we wanted 200 tickets each based on what Sunderland had been promised. To our amazement he agreed there and then, which was particularly surprising as David Wiseman was a member of the FA's Cup Committee.

I dealt with an agent in London who agreed to pay £500 for 50 mixed tickets. I stuck out for £750 for 75, not bad for a ticket that had a face value of 3/6d. Peter Murphy who lived a few doors away from me came in on the transaction.

We were in the Queen's Hotel in Stephenson Place in London when the agent arrived in an open-top white Rolls-Royce. We went for a drink with him and he paid us in white fivers.

Noel Kinsey, who was a tight arse, was reading in the Royal Hotel, Paddington, on the Wednesday lunchtime prior to the Final when I got a call from the agent requesting more tickets. Noel wanted £10 each for his tickets but eventually he settled for a fiver each, so I bought 8 tickets for £40 and sold them on for £60.

The Final Disappointment

Everyone wants to know why we lost the 1956 FA Cup Final as we were red-hot favourites to win. There have been many stories about why we lost: Len Boyd played in a back brace; Trevor Smith had been out late drinking the night before the Final; the shirts were too thick and made of the wrong material, which became heavier as it absorbed sweat; there was resentment in the team that Johnny Newman had been chosen ahead of Jack Badham. None of these factors were true except the thing about the shirts. Manchester City's shirts were short-sleeved, v-necked and made of a lightweight fabric, but our shirts were the complete opposite. They were long-sleeved, so everyone rolled them up, they had collars and were made of typical football shirt cloth that was heavy, retained the heat and sweat and was generally unsuitable for the hot conditions on the day. But the real reason we lost was down to poor man management!

At half-time we were 1–1 and we knew we were a team that was stronger in the second half; however, instead of using the 10 minutes at half time positively a huge row broke out between Arthur Turner and Len Boyd. Arthur came storming in and laid into Len about getting hold of Revie, who had been playing in a deep position for a centre-forward. Len gave as good as he got and the language was disgusting, but it took up the whole of the half-time break. Len was really upset and turned to me and asked 'Am I really playing that bad, Gil?' and that was it, we had lost the opportunity to turn the half-time team talk into one that could have helped us to win the Cup, and it was a de-motivated side that left the Wembley dressing room.

The relationship between Len and Arthur was never healed and when Len did an article for *The People* newspaper, for which he got paid, that was tantamount to handing in his resignation. Len never played another senior game for Birmingham City Football Club.

The Warhurst Issue
Regarding who should have played instead of Roy Warhurst, my choice would have been Johnny Watts because we played Manchester City at Maine Road on 31 March 1956 and John had frightened Revie such that he did not get a kick. We drew the game 1–1, Spud Murphy scoring.

Gil adds: 'Director Bill Dare, at a board meeting after the Final, stated that he had heard the team were in the pay of the bookmakers, an accusation that probably came about as he had had a bet on the Blues to win at 100/1!'

CHAPTER SEVEN
The Manager

Gil's tenure as manager of Birmingham City lasted 47 months, beginning on 1 June 1960 and ending on 30 April 1964. He succeeded Pat Beasley and was replaced by a three-man team headed by Joe Mallet together with Don Dorman and Walter Adams the secretary.

His domestic record per season was:

1960–61

League: 19th in Division One

FA Cup: fifth round replay

League Cup: third round replay

Total: 49 games, 17 wins, 8 draws

1961–62

League: 17th in Division One

FA Cup: third round replay

League Cup: first round replay

Total: 46 games, 14 wins, 12 draws

1962–63

League: 20th in Division One

FA Cup: third round replay

League Cup: winners

Total: 53 games, 16 wins, 17 draws

1963–64

League: 20th in Division One

FA Cup: third round

League Cup: second round

Total: 44 games, 10 wins, 7 draws

This results in a total of 192 games, of which he won 57 (29.6%), drew 44 (22.9%) and lost 91 (47.3%). Add to this his European achievements, and he is without doubt the most successful manager for Birmingham City FC.

The players he utilised as a manager are listed on p117–19 and it is a testimony to his managerial skills and ability to spot a good 'un.

Those players he played alongside who were loyal to him as a manager included John Schofield, Trevor Smith and Graham Sissons, who played for Gil 84, 162 and 71 times respectively. The players he brought into the club proved to be top performers, too. They included Mike Hellawell (172 appearances), Jimmy Bloomfield (140 appearances), Jimmy Harris (108 appearances), Bertie Auld (123 appearances), Stan Lynn (102 appearances), Ken Leek (104 appearances) and Colin Green (57 appearances in two seasons).

He was never afraid to give youngsters their chance, and the following players who grew up with the club made their debuts for Gil: Malcolm Beard, Colin Withers, Terry Hennessey, Dennis Thwaites, Brian Sharples, Greg Farrell, John Regan, Brian Rushton, Trevor Wolstenholme, Geoff Anderson, Ray Martin, Winston Foster and Johnny Vincent.

Brian Sharples recalls how he heard about his debut: I had travelled with the first team to Sheffield to help out and learn, there were no substitutes in those days so a few of the younger pros were invited to go along. I was just 18 on 15 September 1962, as my birthday was 6 September, and we had been beaten 5–0 by Wednesday. I was sitting at the front of the coach near the driver when Gil approached me, put his hand on my knee and said, "Do you fancy a game on Wednesday night?" I asked him what he meant and [he said] he was giving me my debut against Albion. It was typical of Gil, no-nonsense, matter-of-fact and decisive. All the qualities you need to be a great goalkeeper and manager. I was on cloud nine and could look forward and plan for the greatest day in my football career.

Trevor Wolstenholme recalls: 'The Boss' came in as manager in the early 1960s, which as you are probably aware was not only the beginning of the cultural revolution, but also a changing time for football with the end of the maximum wage. He introduced lots of new ideas to the club such as the weighing of players and updated the medical side. He also signed a Spanish coach, Emilio Aldecoa, to coach the younger players. He was also very tactically astute, thus belying the myth that goalkeepers do not make good managers.

I suppose my most everlasting memory of 'The Boss' would be his sheer physical presence. Whenever he came into the dressing room at half-time or full-time of a match that hadn't gone so well, he would stand there in his camel hair overcoat, his face blood red, and he was a giant of a man, he absolutely filled the room so those of us who hadn't been quick enough to get down the tunnel and into the toilets were left to sit there and tremble while he vented his fury. As a man, I liked 'The Boss', he was always fair and honest with me, although I did not always appreciate it at the time, and he also had a good sense of humour when the occasion warranted it.

Winston Foster remembers: Gil was always willing to give the players that were younger a chance if the circumstances were right to do so.

I was given my first-team debut in the first leg of the Inter-Cities Fairs Cup Final at home to FC Roma, which we drew 2–2. That sort of chance gives you a boost to your confidence that you appreciate.

v FC Roma, 27 September 1961   **Drew 2–2**

Blues: Schofield, Farmer, Sissons, Hennessey, Foster, Beard, Hellawell, Bloomfield, Harris, Orritt, Auld.

Attendance: 21,005
Scorers: Hellawell, Orritt

Another memory was of the second leg in Rome. I was sitting on the bench with the other players and Gil. There was friction on the pitch which was then transferred to the bench; suddenly Gil and the Roma manager were off their benches and marching towards one another. When the Roma manager got close to Gil and suddenly realised the size that Gil was he did an about-

turn and went straight back to his bench and sat down again. We were in hysterics for minutes afterwards.

Colin Green recalls: When I was a lad I used to collect cigarette cards of footballers, and the famous Gil Merrick was one that I treasured as he was one of my footballing heroes. So when I was asked to join Blues in December 1962 the decision was made a lot easier because Gil was the manager.

You could never take liberties with Gil, he was fair and honest and what I would call a player's manager, he was absolutely fantastic at sticking up for the players. It was an absolute shock when he left and the whole episode was a disgrace.

I remember playing against Fulham at Craven Cottage in May 1963 and I scored a cracking goal, but at the wrong end! In those days the directors seats were in a sort of balcony right by me. As the ball fizzed past Colin Withers I felt the wrath from the balcony, I looked at Terry Hennessey's face and feared the worst. When I got back in the dressing room at half-time Gil came over to me and very calmly said, 'You weren't thinking then, get your head straight and concentrate on the second half.' No swearing, throwing tea or hairdryers! The game finished 3–3.

The players Gil utilised while he was manager

Number	Player	1960–61	1961–62	1962–63	1963–64	Total
1	Schofield	19	39	22	4	84
2	Farmer	48	10	0	1	59
3	Allen	45	6	0	0	51
4	Watts	36	5	18	0	59
5	Smith	37	43	46	36	162
6	Neal	46	7	0	0	53
7	Astall	20	0	0	0	20

Number	Player	1960–61	1961–62	1962–63	1963–64	Total
8	Gordon	26	0	0	0	26
9	Weston	7	0	0	0	7
10	Rudd	18	2	0	0	20
11	Hooper	10	0	0	0	10
12	Stubbs	13	8	15	0	36
13	Beard	4	46	43	38	131
14	Singer	23	3	0	0	26
15	Sissons	15	36	20	0	71
16	Hellawell	34	46	51	41	172
17	Barlow	6	0	0	0	6
18	Orritt	14	19	0	0	33
19	Taylor	22	4	0	0	26
20	Withers	30	7	31	40	108
21	Bloomfield	30	37	37	36	140
22	Harris	24	42	37	5	108
23	Hennessey	10	37	52	41	140
24	Foster	2	15	6	14	37
25	Auld	0	41	47	35	123
26	Lynn	0	26	42	34	102
27	Leek	0	26	50	28	104
28	Wright	0	2	0	0	2
29	Bullock P.	0	1	15	11	27
30	Thwaites	0	1	6	10	17
31	Sharples	0	0	4	0	4
32	Regan	0	0	4	3	7
33	Farrell	0	0	2	3	5
34	Green	0	0	22	35	57
35	Rushton	0	0	11	4	15

Number	Player	1960–61	1961–62	1962–63	1963–64	Total
36	Wolstenholme	0	0	2	0	2
37	Harley	0	0	0	24	24
38	Thomson	0	0	0	22	22
39	Martin	0	0	0	14	14
40	Anderson	0	0	0	1	1
41	Bullock M.	0	0	0	2	2
42	Vincent	0	0	0	2	2

As Gil described in Chapter One, he was thrust into management with only 12 months experience 'looking after the youngsters'. He was forced to learn as he went along, drawing upon the experiences of his two major influences, Harry Storer and Bob Brocklebank.

Harry was a good judge of character. After I had become manager at Blues I went to watch a pre-season testimonial game at Derby. After the game I went into the guest lounge and Harry was there. He came over to me and said, 'Who the f*****g hell do you think you are to manage that club with all those b******s?' The directors never liked Harry because he always put the players ahead of them, even when we were getting on a coach he would put his arm across the waiting directors to allow the players on first.

Harry taught me a lot about how to handle players when they got too big for their boots. I had gashed my thumb opening a can at home and I was unfit for two games. When I was available to play I expected to go straight back into the team, but Harry Storer stuck with Jackie Wheeler and I was in the reserves. When I challenged Harry about this he said that Wheeler had been playing well and since the team had been in good form he decided to leave it alone.

My pride was hurt and we argued and then he tried to 'flannel' me to get out of the row, suggesting that I had not been up to form recently and suggesting a fault in part of my game. I knew this was not true but I finished the argument with the comment, 'I see, that's it; that's finished me.'

I played seven games for the reserves and did not concede a goal. It was always my style to play as hard and as well as I could no matter at what level. For me that was the true definition of a professional. However, during that period I was feeling low and decided to ask for a transfer. I had learnt that players, no matter how important, were never bigger than the club – a valuable lesson.

The board refused my request and while nothing made the papers I know that Villa heard about my unrest and made enquiries in a bid to get me, but Blues refused to listen to any offers.

Bob Brocklebank took over early in 1949 and he and Storer were like chalk and cheese; Storer forceful, aggressive and outspoken, Bob quiet, retiring and less vigorous in his approach to players.

Another major difference was their attitude to the transfer market. Storer only bought Jackie Stewart from Raith Rovers for a couple of thousand pounds, while in his first five years Brocklebank spent £160,000 on players but received as much, if not more, in return for players he had sold. He was a shrewd operator, the best salesman in football. When Bob took over at Blues we were essentially a defensive side, but he changed the style and introduced the attacking type of player through his transfer policy.

I guess I was a hybrid of the two, preferring home-grown talent but if it was not good enough I was more than prepared to go to the transfer market.

Bob Brocklebank's transfer dealings

Player	Bought From	Sold To
Bill Robertson		Stoke City 1952
Walter Quinton		Brentford 1949
Tony Blake		Gillingham 1952
Neil Dougall		Plymouth 1949
Martin McDonnell		Coventry 1949
Ray Ferris		Worcester City 1953
John Berry		Manchester United 1951
Bobby Brennan		Fulham 1950
Ted Purdon	Maritz Brothers South Africa 1950	Sunderland 1954
Tommy Capel	Chesterfield 1949	Nottingham Forest 1949
Willie Wardle	Blackpool 1951	Barnsley 1953
Don Dorman		Coventry 1951
Frank McKee		Gillingham 1952
Ted Duckhouse		Northampton 1950
Bill Smith	Northampton 1950	Blackburn 1952
Jack Goodwin		Brentford 1949
Jim Dailey	Sheffield Wednesday 1949	Exeter City 1952
Tommy Briggs	Coventry 1951	Blackburn 1952
Harold Bodle		Bury 1949
Harold Roberts		Shrewsbury 1951
Bob Laing		Watford 1950
Fred Slater		York City 1951
John Jordan	Juventus, Italy 1949	Sheffield Wednesday 1950
Bill Havenga		Luton 1950
James Higgins	Dundalk 1949	Dundalk 1952
Ted O'Hara	Dundalk 1949	Hereford 1951

Merrick's Major signings

Player	Price	Date
Jimmy Bloomfield	£30,000	November 1960
Jimmy Harris	£20,000	December 1960
Bertie Auld	£15,000	April 1961
Stan Lynn	£500	October 1961
Ken Leek	£23,000	November 1961
Colin Green	£12,000	December 1962
Alex Harley	£42,500	August 1963

Debutants who had significant careers

Johnny Vincent: 190 + 4 appearances, 44 goals.
Sold to Middlesbrough for £40,000, March 1971.

Terry Hennessey: 203 appearances, 3 goals.
Sold to Nottingham Forest for £70,000, November 1965.

Malcolm Beard: 403 + 2 appearances, 33 goals.

Colin Withers: 116 appearances.
Sold to Villa for £18,000, November 1964.

Total transfer dealings resulted in a loss of £16,500: in, £144,500 and out, £128,000.

It has often been reported that Gil was the first manager to open up with a European Final, and that his first task was to prepare the team for the European Inter-Cities Fairs Cup Final second leg, away to Barcelona.

Gil remembers: No my first game as manager was the opening game of the 1960–61 against Bolton at Burden Park, which we drew 2–2.

Alex Harley was first spotted by Gil when he was playing for Third Lanark: It was my first season in charge, and Walter Adams the secretary had received a request through the Football Association for us to tour Canada in the summer of 1961. It was a great experience. We started off against Third Lanark at the Polo Grounds in New York, a game we lost 4–1 before starting the tour in Montreal where we lost 1–0 against Cantalia. Having lost our first two games, we never lost a game after those reversals. We beat Hamilton Stealers in Ontario 4–2, Third Lanark in Toronto 3–2 and Calgary All-Stars in Calgary 11–2 (I went on as centre-forward and scored two, they weren't the most difficult of opponents!). After drawing with Third Lanark 1–1 in Vancouver, we stayed in that city to beat the British Columbia All-Stars 5–2, a game in which I blooded the youngsters; Malcolm Beard and Terry Hennessey, 19 and 18 [years old] respectively. Our final game was in Toronto where we beat Rheims 2–1.

The only player to cause me a problem was Harley – that I didn't expect. Don Dorman had been sent to Spain to 'spy' on Alex. His report gave Alex a clean bill of health; he played football on the beach everyday and had early nights. On that basis I agreed to play £42,500 to Manchester City for his services. We'd given Alex a back-hander of a grand to sign, which was provided in cash in the proverbial brown paper bag, all organised by David Wiseman, a member of the FA. Anyway Don and I had agreed to meet Alex in Manchester and bring him back to St Andrew's in our car. When we got to the rendezvous, Alex was there in his new cream Ford Zephyr, which you could buy in those days for less than a thousand pounds. So he followed us to the ground to play in a pre-season friendly against an Irish team. At St Andrew's I asked Alex to give his boots to our trainer, Ken Fish. I was amazed that a professional footballer had not got his boots with him, and we fixed him up with a second-hand pair. We won the game by about four goals and Alex missed every opportunity he had. Ken and I consoled ourselves that at least he was in a position to score, but we had our suspicions. When he took his boots off his feet were red with blood. Not the best start for a new signing.

Alex continued to miss chance after chance and in the end I started leaving him out – I had no choice – and it coincided with him visiting nightclubs on a Friday night. He really let me down.

Jimmy Harris recalls: Gil was reported to have said about me that if I'd been married I would have played for England. I always liked a pretty girl and in fact when I did eventually get married it was to Joan Boardman who was Miss England in 1960.

After I made my debut for Everton in 1955 I had always been able to score against Blues and often Gil was in goal so it was no surprise when he came to sign me. He always had the knack of finding the right players to fit in to his team, imagine the forward line we had in 1963 – Hellawell, Bloomfield, me, Ken Leek and Bertie Auld. He liked to sign players who knew the game, all that forward line were signed in their mid to late 20s. We were good mates.

I fell out with Gil when he went behind my back, as I saw it, and signed Alex Harley as my replacement. Alex first appeared on the scene in Canada playing for Third Lanark, and it was obvious that Gil thought he was a good player.

In my opinion goalkeepers do not make good managers as players do not give them the respect.

Returning to Alex Harley, I remember Fishy [Ken Fish] had given us the bank holiday off and we were due in for training on the following morning, but Alex didn't show until the afternoon when he turned up in a flash car with a bird leaning out the window. Gil went mad!

Alex definitely let Gil down and was partly the cause of him getting the sack.

On 11 January 1964 we were away at Manchester United, so I told Ken Fish, my trainer, that I was going to get Alex Harley out of the drinking clubs and surround him with kids. I told Alex, who had not delivered for me since I signed him, that he was a hero at Manchester City and he should get out and show them at Old Trafford what he could do. The team was:

Player	Date of Birth	Age
Colin Withers	21 March 1940	23
Stan Lynn	18 June 1928	35
Ray Martin	23 January 1945	18
Terry Hennessey	1 September 1942	21
Trevor Smith	13 April 1936	27
Malcolm Beard	3 May 1942	21
Geoff Anderson	26 November 1944	19
Alex Harley	20 April 1936	27
Mick Bullock	2 October 1946	17
Bobby Thomson	21 March 1937	36
Bertie Auld	23 March 1938	26

On Friday afternoon I set up a practice game for the team for Saturday against the rest. Up in the stands was one of the directors, Mr Richards. After the practice was over he asked me which team I was playing the next day, to which I replied, 'You have just seen them.' He didn't say a word and left. The following morning we were leaving at 9am and, apart from the players and my staff, there was no one, no directors or the usual hangers-on who, when we went to Old Trafford, made the journey to Manchester as it was normally considered a bit of a perk. No one wished us good luck, I was on my own. After 10 minutes Harley scored to make it 1–0 then Denis Law equalised before Mick Bullock scored the winner. I sat in the stands and Matt Busby came over to me and said, 'Gil the kids have done it for you.' The crowd that day was 44,695.

The week previous we had lost 4–1 to Arsenal at home, and from the team I dropped Green, Hellawell, Bloomfield and Leek. That was Geoff Anderson's only first-team appearance.

Despite some dark times, Gil has fond memories of his time as manager. One event in particular that stands out for him involves Bertie Auld.

Gil remembers: One funny incident was what happened to Bertie Auld. Bertie had just joined the club and he kept complaining about his thigh muscle after the first two games. Our physiotherapist could not locate the problem but Bertie was still moaning. I said to Ken Fish 'get a top class physio in and let's get him sorted.' Ken found one and we decided to treat Bertie in my room. When Bertie arrived the physio laid him on the bed and gave him a full examination and afterwards prescribed a course of injections. On hearing that, Bertie jumped off the bed and refused the treatment. I said 'Bertie we've got to get you right for next season, you've got to have it done.' Well even I felt sorry for him. The physio laid him on the bed and proceeded to put six needles into his thigh in a line. Bertie was moaning and shouting in agony before the physio had started. Once the blood started to come out of the needles, the physio applied syringes of drugs and pumped them into his thigh. He must have been in agony, but I thought to myself, that'll teach him to keep complaining. We sent him home the next day. Did it work? Well he never moaned again and went on to play 147 games scoring 31 goals. What a character!

Bertie remembers it in a slightly different way however. He recalls: When we were touring North America I developed a problem in my left thigh and I was diagnosed as requiring an immediate cortisone injection. I recall Gil and Ken Fish having to hold me down as this Russian doctor proceeded to inject me in four different places! I went home early and was ready for the start of the season thanks to Gil ensuring that I received the best possible treatment both in America and on my return to the Midlands.

Gil's travels around North America and Canada led him to write an article in *Charles Buchan's Football Monthly* in October 1961 entitled 'Soccer in Canada – it is growing but the crowd want goals and thrills – not science'. Last summer I had one of the most enjoyable experiences in my soccer life when I toured Canada with Birmingham City at the invitation of the Canadian FA. Although what I saw and learned must be considered purely in the light of our own club performances, I could not help but be impressed by the vast potential.

The Canadian Association officials are anxious to win Canadians over to the game. And I don't necessarily mean those only of British and French stock, whose forefathers were the early colonists, but also the cosmopolitan population of the East coast where European immigration is probably at its highest.

Like its neighbour, the United States, Canada is becoming a cosmopolitan country. Because of that I believe soccer over there has a greater chance than ever before.

Admittedly ice hockey has not forfeited any of its popularity as a major Canadian sport – and I do not think it will – but baseball is losing ground and so is American 'grid-iron' football, both to soccer.

Unless, however, the Canadian officials change their policy of encouraging too many financially-sponsored 'artificial' tournaments and Leagues, the game will not make the stride forward it should.

What they need most of all are qualified coaches who are prepared to dedicate themselves to the game.

Because the Canadian officials are so eager to 'sell' soccer to a sporting population which has been reared largely on the concentrated thrills and spills of ice hockey and the 'grid-iron' game, they are inclined to cater for crowds which expect the same from soccer.

Canadian fans want goals and yet more goals. Above all they expect to see plenty of excitement and toughness for their dollars. If a 'rough house' develops, well that is all the better.

With this in mind the Canadians have obtained several players from Southern and Central American countries in the mistaken belief that these imports – well-paid of course – will show the crowds the real arts and crafts of the game.

But as we found in our first Canadian tour game against a team called Cantalia, at Montreal, these players are third-raters who cannot command regular places in the better clubs within their own countries.

We expected an exhibition game for our first match. The idea, we thought, was to show the crowd how English-style soccer could and should be played with the results not all that important.

Our opponents – and the home crowd – had very different ideas. The game developed into a shambles. Our lads were not allowed to play football. It was clear that for the rest of the tour we would have to play to win. That was the least that was expected of us.

As far as the Canadians were concerned – especially in the East – prestige was at stake. If their local teams could beat us the crowds would flock to see other games, and soccer's popularity as a mass spectator sport would boom.

We lost the opening Montreal game 0–1 and then moved on to play Hamilton Steelers in Ontario. There we met wonderful enthusiasm, tremendous hospitality from a population essentially Scottish in character – and a far better standard of football. We won 4–2.

In Toronto, where Danny Blanchflower, Johnny Haynes and Stanley Matthews were 'appearing for a season' we played the only other British club on tour – Third Lanark. The Scottish First Division club had beaten us 4–1 in the Polo Grounds in New York, but this time we won 3–2 after a fine exhibition of soccer from both clubs.

Yet the Canadians were disappointed because more goals had not been scored.

In that match, our goalkeeper, Colin Withers, and the Third Lanark goalkeeper, Robertson, played 'blinders'. I am afraid the Canadians overlooked that!

In Calgary we met former England half-back Bert Mozley who now manages two prosperous hotels. We repaid his grand hospitality by whipping his Calgary All-Stars 11–2, I went on at centre-forward in the second-half of this pleasant match and scored twice!

The 'rubber' match with Third Lanark ended in a 1–1 draw in Vancouver – again the local press expected more goals. Then we got down to preparing for the highlight of the tour – the match in Vancouver's Empire Stadium against the formidable British Columbia All-Stars.

The All-Stars, an all-Canadian team, were the crack outfit. They had defeated Tottenham Hotspur and West Bromwich Albion on previous tours and the leading Scottish clubs which had toured the country. They were unbeaten since 1956.

Such was the volume of pre-match publicity and propaganda about this game, and the multitude of warnings from well-meaning friends who told us not to underestimate the opposition, that I decided on some special training.

It paid off. We gave what was afterwards described by the always generous British Colombians as the greatest show by any touring side and beat the All-Stars 5–2. Jimmy Bloomfield and Mike Hellawell were in brilliant form and the All-Stars could not stop them.

They played good football, but in a very open, old-fashioned English style, with their big bustling centre-forward their danger man. But Trevor

Smith cut him out of the game from the start, and I was rather disappointed to see that our much-vaunted opponents appeared to have no other plan.

Their football, like so many of the teams we played, lacked imagination and tactical resource. That is why I say the Canadians need experienced coaches not 'exhibition' players who do not contribute anything at all of lasting benefit.

This display against the All-Stars was matched only by the game we played as an 'extra' against the French League Champions, Rheims, in Toronto. We won 2–1 and delighted a big crowd.

In all we played eight matches on our 14,000-mile round trip, won five and scored 29 goals. Everywhere we went we were made welcome, even in Toronto after that first unfortunate game, and everywhere we found enthusiasm, good dressing room accommodation, first rate medical and training facilities and, except where baseball pitches overlapped, good playing pitches.

The crowds in Canada were quite good by our standards – 14,000 was the biggest gate we drew – but on the other hand I didn't see a single player of outstanding ability.

I have said that soccer interest is greater in the East just now, but the game is more likely to flourish in the West.

There the people have a deeper, more dedicated attitude – an attitude which is concerned not so much with trying to put soccer over as a 'spectacle' but in getting the public interested in it as a science and as an entertaining sport, which is what it is meant to be.

I like to think that my club, Birmingham City, were able to contribute something towards that ideal, and that we have not visited that great country for the last time.

North America Tour, May–June 1961
Played 9, Won 6, Drew 1, Lost 2, For 32, Against 16.

Date	Opposition	Location	Result	Score
17 May	Third Lanark	New York	Lost	1–4
21 May	Montreal Cantalia	Montreal	Lost	0–1
25 May	Hamilton Stealers	Hamilton	Won	4–2
27 May	Third Lanark	Toronto	Won	3–2
30 May	Calgary All-Stars	Calgary	Won	11–2
3 June	Third Lanark	Vancouver	Drew	1–1
7 June	Victoria All-Stars	Victoria	Won	5–1
10 June	British Columbia All-Stars	Vancouver	Won	5–2
14 June	FC Rheims	Toronto	Won	2–1

The 1963 League Cup Win

Gil's team won the League Cup Final in 1963 – 45 years on this is still the only major trophy Birmingham City have won!

They did things differently in 1963. This was the year they shot an American president, the year they deified a pop group and the year that fashion gurus devised a standard that made drainpipe trousers compulsory attire. The whole world was in transition, and even football, then a means of escape for the working classes, was unsure of its role in society. Everton won the League, Manchester United the FA Cup and George Best moved from Belfast to Old Trafford. When Blues played Villa in the League Cup Final first leg at St Andrew's that May they could not sell out the stadium. Such a scenario would be unthinkable today, but in 1963 Britain was a cold place, constrained by recession and not yet ready to embrace a competition that was ignored by the top clubs. The League Cup suffered from an identity crisis. Readers who shelled out three old pence for *The Birmingham Post* on Tuesday 23 May would not have been surprised to find that the report of the second leg at Villa Park was not even the most substantial story. 'League Cup draw earns Blues their first major honour' was the headline, but the match report by Cyril Chapman was inexplicably smaller than the article for the Kent versus Warwickshire cricket match at Gravesend. Charlie Aitken was not complaining. The owner of the thickest head of hair in the game, Aitken was a young defender who, like many of his Villa teammates, wondered what the hell the League Cup was all about. In those days there was no direct entry into Europe and no prize money. The two encounters in the League Cup Final are more important now than they were then. Whenever opposing fans taunt Bluenoses with chants of 'you've never won f*** all' they miss the point about 1963.

John Schofield was baffled why the competition was deemed to be so irrelevant: We found this strange as it had been such a big thing when Villa won it in 1961. We had a good team. Our playmaker was Jimmy Bloomfield who had been persuaded to come out of London to join us following a spell at Arsenal. He was responsible for improving the skill of Mike Hellawell who was a fast-raiding winger.

There has been much talk regarding how important the League Cup was in 1963. Of the 22 teams in the First Division in the 1962–63 season only 11 entered the competition, those which did not enter were: Everton (first), Spurs (second), Burnley (third), Wolves (fifth), Sheffield Wednesday (sixth), Arsenal (seventh), Liverpool (eighth), Nottingham Forest (ninth), West Bromwich Albion (14th), Ipswich (17th), Manchester United (19th).

The sides that did enter were: Leicester City (fourth), Sheffield United

(10th), Blackburn (11th), West Ham (12th), Blackpool (13th), Aston Villa (15th), Fulham (16th), Bolton Wanderers (18th), Manchester City (21st), Leyton Orient (22nd).

The Road to Victory

First round

Bye

Second round

2 September v Doncaster Rovers (h) won 5–0

Scorers: Leek 2, Bloomfield, Harris, Auld.

Third round

3 October v Barrow (a) drew 1–1

Scorers: Wolstenholme

Third round replay

29 October v Barrow (h) won 5–1

Scorers: Harris 2, Stubbs, Leek, Arrowsmith (og).

Fourth round

14 November v Notts County (h) won 3–2

Scorers: Lynn (pen), Harris, Auld.

Fifth round

11 December v Manchester City (h) won 6–0

Scorers: Lynn 2 (1 pen), Leek, Auld, Leivers (opp own-goal), Sear (og).

Semi-final first leg

27 March v Bury (h) won 3–2

Scorers: Bullock, Leek, Auld.

Semi-final second leg

8 April v Bury (a) drew 1–1

Scorers: Leek

Final v Aston Villa, 23 May 1963   **Won 3–1**

Blues: Schofield, Lynn, Green, Hennessey, Smith, Beard, Hellawell, Bloomfield, Harris, Leek, Auld.

Scorers: Leek 2, Bloomfield.

Final second leg v Aston Villa, 27 May 1963   **Drew 0–0**

Won 3–1 on aggregate

Blues: Schofield, Lynn, Green, Hennessey, Smith, Beard, Hellawell, Bloomfield, Harris, Leek, Auld.

The Match Report

The 1963 League Cup Final was Blues' first domestic final in seven years and one they simply had to win because the opposition were their neighbours and rivals, Aston Villa. Blues went into the match as the underdogs, having been beaten by Villa just two months previously in a League match by 4–0. Both sides started at full strength in front of a St Andrew's crowd of 31,580.

Blues started well with close efforts from Harris and Leek, both well saved by Sims in goal for Villa. Blues best chance came soon after another shot from Harris was pushed onto the crossbar by Sims. Meanwhile, Thomson clattered Blues 'keeper Schofield in a rash challenge for the ball and in another incident Leek sent Crowe flying with a late tackle, both fouls coming in the early stages of a typically keenly fought local derby. Then the first goal came and to the joy of the home fans it was scored by Ken Leek on 14 minutes. A ball from midfield by Harris released Auld and his left-wing cross was hammered in by Leek; this time Sims had no chance of saving it.

Bloomfield became the first casualty, leaving to have a thigh wound bandaged up, and he returned to spend time hobbling on the wing in order to try and run the knock off. He did so successfully, much to the relief of the Blues fans and management. However, Villa soon got back into the game and equalised through Thomson. Lee started the move, and after advancing deep into Blues territory he sent in a hard, low cross which Thomson hit first time and it sped past Schofield as he was coming out to close the Villa man down.

The second half started badly for Villa. Defender Sleeuwenhoek collided with his goalkeeper and ended up with an injury which he had to leave the field to have treated. Soon after that Blues had a man off too when Smith was hurt in a hefty challenge by Thomson. The first real opportunity at goal was converted and it put Blues back in front on 52 minutes. Again Harris and Auld were the instigators and Leek the goalscorer, with a low drive within the area from Auld's inch-perfect cross.

The game became ill-tempered and referee Crawford was starting to lose patience with the persistent fouling. Crowe became another victim when he was elbowed in the face after a midfield tussle with Auld. Aitken was then given a stern lecture when he was seen to shove Hellawell away in yet another confrontation. Then Fraser and Harris came close to exchanging punches as they squared up to one another and teammates had to drag them apart, earning them a warning from the Doncaster official. Blues then got a killer third goal after 66 minutes. From a Harris right-wing cross, Bloomfield nipped in unchecked by the static defence to squeeze the ball past Sims and in off the post. Blues were now 3–1 up and they confidently strolled through the remainder of the game, content to take their lead to Villa Park for the second leg. In the closing stages Sims saved Villa, keeping out two glorious strikes at goal from Leek and then Auld. The final whistle went with Blues still holding a two-goal advantage.

The second leg was held on 27 May 1963 and was a massive anti-climax, with the Blues' stifling Villa in a goalless draw.

It is a mystery how Blues won, but they did produce perhaps their most impressive display of that season to win the first leg 3–1 at St Andrew's in front of 31,580 people. Blues served up a treat of attacking football, taking the lead through Leek in the 14th minute and controlling the game with such assurance that their supporters must have wondered why the team had performed so badly in the First Division. Villa equalised through Thomson but were no match for their opponents. Leek scored again in the 52nd minute and Bloomfield made it 3–1 in the 66th. The second leg at Villa Park four nights later attracted 37,921 but was an anticlimax. Villa did not have the craft to stage a fightback and Blues, eager to protect their lead rather than add to it, spent most of the match kicking the ball out for throw-ins. The tactic worked and by the start of the 1963–64 season Blues were able to distribute photographs of their team sitting proudly on benches with the trophy in the foreground.

Gil remembers: We had struggled a bit in the League and the Final came when the season was over. I think the rivalry between us and the Villa made it a special occasion. Our defence was very good. We had Johnny Schofield in goal and Stan Lynn and Colin Green as our full-backs. Stan, from the Villa, was the best buy I ever made. He was an outstanding player and a great personality. Our half-back line consisted of Terry Hennessey, Trevor Smith and Malcolm Beard, two of whom came up through the junior ranks. The forward line included Mick Hellawell, Ken Leek, Jimmy Harris, Jimmy Bloomfield and Bertie Auld. It was a memorable victory for us. It's amazing to think that the club has not been to a major final since, but that's the way football is, isn't it?

1963 League Cup winning team

Player	Apps	Gls	Seasons
Schofield	237	0	14
Lynn	148	30	5
Green	217	1	9
Hennessey	202	3	6
Smith	430	3	12
Beard	403/2	32	11
Hellawell	213	33	8
Bloomfield	148	32	4
Harris	115	53	4
Leek	120	61	4
Auld	145	31	5

The 1963 League Cup winning team – where did they go?

Player	Destination
Johnny Schofield	Wrexham 1966
Stan Lynn	Stourbridge 1966
Colin Green	Wrexham 1971
Terry Hennessey	Nottingham Forest 1965
Trevor Smith	Walsall 1964
Malcolm Beard	Aston Villa 1971
Mick Hellawell	Sunderland 1965
Jimmy Bloomfield	Brentford 1964
Jimmy Harris	Oldham 1964
Ken Leek	Northampton 1964
Bertie Auld	Glasgow Celtic 1965

A League Apart by Malcolm Stent

BLUES legend and former manager Gil Merrick has only been to St Andrew's once in 42 years. But he'll be on stage at the Alexandra Theatre next week recalling how he helped to win the club's only major trophy during its 100-year history at the ground.

From Tuesday, he'll help to kick-off every performance of Malcolm Stent's play *A League Apart* during its five-day run.

The play features a girl from a rich, Catholic family of Villa fans in Sutton Coldfield meeting a relatively poor, Protestant Blues' fan from Small Heath.

It's based around the two-leg 1963 League Cup Final, when the former England goalkeeper was Birmingham City's manager during their victory over local rivals Villa.

He has done question and answer sessions in public before, but nothing quite as grand as opening a play – which he'll do with the help of BBC WM late show presenter Jimmy Franks.

Gil has already talked about how his managerial career ended at the very beginning of the book, but reprinted below is the newspaper report by Peter Ingall from the *Daily Mirror* on Wednesday 29 April.

MERRICK SACKED AFTER 25 YEARS

A twenty-five year era ended yesterday when Birmingham City asked their manager, Gil Merrick, to resign.

Merrick, who found fame as England's goalkeeper but never reached the same starry heights as a manager, was axed just three days after Birmingham had escaped relegation for the fourth time in five years.

He is the fifth Birmingham manager forced to resign since the war and the first victim of the club's promised facelift – a 'new look' they hope will lift them from the seemingly permanent spot at the bottom of the First Division.

But the sacking of Merrick – strictly a one-club man – was a difficult decision to make. Vice-chairman and FA Councillor David Wiseman said: 'It was a hard thing to do because Merrick was great as a player and a man. But this time we've had to put the good of the club before personal reasons.'

Merrick was told of the board's decision after a special meeting at the ground. He drove away from St Andrew's without a word to the players...and away from a club he had served for 25 years.

A local boy, he joined the Birmingham ground staff in August 1939. After the war he established himself as regular first-team goalkeeper and twice helped the club to First Division promotion.

Merrick won his first England cap in 1951 and reigned as No. 1 goalkeeper for three years, making 23 international appearances.

He ended his playing career in May 1960 and took over as Birmingham manager a month later.

But his record since then has not been impressive. In the last four seasons Birmingham have finished 19th, 17th, 20th and 20th in the First Division, having twice escaped relegation by two points and last Saturday by one.

Merrick said: 'We had had a bad season and the board of directors decided that a change was needed. It was one of those things but I was very bitter about it at the time. I had always wanted to go into management after I finished my playing career and it was even more special to do that at the club that I had actually played at for so many years. I really enjoyed it and what gave me the most satisfaction was to watch young apprentices like Terry Hennessey, Malcolm Beard, Malcolm Page and Johnny Vincent come through into the first team. We had a few players like that come through the system and I took pride in that. We won the League Cup and reached the Final of the Inter-Cities Fairs Cup in 1960 and 1961. We were the pioneers for English football in Europe.'

'If this is what the club want I must abide by it. I'm not particularly surprised. I don't suppose anyone came into management at a more difficult time than I did, but I would like to stay in the game.'

Within hours of Merrick agreeing to the board's request the names of Northampton manager Dave Bowen and former Sheffield Wednesday chief Vic Buckingham were being strongly linked with the vacancy. Meanwhile secretary Walter Adams and assistant manager Don Dorman will share the manager's duties.

But Merrick's departure is likely to be only the first of the expected upheaval at St Andrew's.

Vice-chairman Wiseman added: 'Because of our record over the past five years we want to start from scratch again.'

For the record, the following season, 1964–65, with Joe Mallet as manager, Blues finished 22nd in the First Division and were relegated to Division Two, where they spent seven seasons before being promoted to Division One in 1971–72.

Managerial Q & A

 Which players impressed you during your time as Blues manager?

Mike Hellawell, a religious Yorkshireman who never let me down and we worked hard on his pace and crossing. I like to think I helped him get his England cap.

Mike recalls: I signed for the Blues in 1957 while I was doing my National Service. When I came out of the army in 1959 I think Gil had retired so I don't remember him as the great goalkeeper that he most certainly was. I did, however, see him play cricket many times and am convinced he could have gone a long way in the game if he hadn't concentrated on football. I remember the time he played up at Harrogate against a very strong Yorkshire League team in a testimonial match. He hit a magnificent fifty, and some of his hook shots were quite fearsome.

As a manager I think his record gets better as time goes on as when he left Blues they were in the top division. Since then they have been relegated quite a few times, and of course he was in charge when we won the League Cup in 1963. When he took over as manager he put me straight into the first team and within two years I was selected for England, so he'd still be in charge if it was up to me.

As a man he was exemplary. If I was on trial for my life I would pick Gil to be my judge. I couldn't speak too highly of him as I always looked up to him as a father figure.

● The late **John Schofield**, for so long my deputy when playing – he was top-bracket.

● **Terry Hennessey**, I was working at S & U when Terry came to see me, saying, 'Boss they're offering me money to join Nottingham Forest. What should I do?' I advised him to leave but they should have built a team around Terry.

By the way he always called me 'Boss' – even after he and I had finished our playing careers.

● **Malcolm Page**, what a lovely man, I signed him as a boy and he is still a friend today.

- **Winston Foster,** who, until he recently got a new knee, used to come over from Kidderminster to do my garden every Tuesday while I was not so good.

- **Graham Sissons,** a 100 per cent player and man.

Graham recalls: I first met Gil in 1952 when I was with the Youth Team on tour in Zurich. It was the last match of the tour and was the pre-match game prior to the full international of Switzerland against England. After the match we were sitting around the touchline when he came up to us and had a chat, it was quite a thrill to meet an England international.

I played with Gil and was also managed by him. I also played cricket with him for S & U Ltd. Gil worked there in personnel and there were a few ex-Blues players employed as travellers, including me, Cyril Trigg and Len Boyd.

Gil ran the Blues cricket team and we had some good players. As well as me and Gil there was Mike Hellawell, Brian Orritt and Robin Stubbs.

Gil was a great 'keeper, he commanded the area and dominated things which is just what you need from a goalie. He was easy to get on with and was always helpful, he would take you to one side and have a chat in an attempt to get you to play a bit better.

I recall one pre-season, Ken Fish was a fitness fanatic and the whole week had been building up to the Saturday morning road run which was approximately 20 miles around the training ground at Elmdon. I was running with Maurice Partridge who had a groin strain and I had sore feet so we were well behind. Anyway we got as far as The Clock pub on the Coventry Road and were heading back when suddenly we heard a noise in the bushes, it sounded like a grizzly bear, and out of the bushes came Gil who had decided to take a shortcut. He was sweating profusely and covered in leaves and stuff. Normally he looked like Clark Gable but on this occasion he was more like Worzel Gummidge.'

What has been your funniest moment?

One player I remember was Bertie Auld, he was always up and down, saying things like, 'I don't know whether I'll be fit or not.' He invariably was in the end. He was a fiery character and I recall a game against Fulham when Johnny Haynes had spat at him so Bertie laid him out. Haynes was out for a week and his colleague Maurice Cook, who was a big lad, came over and Bertie sorted him out too. Cook was out for three weeks and Bertie was sent off. I can also remember him jumping up to try and give Ron Yeats, Liverpool's giant centre-half, a 'Glasgow Kiss'.

 Who do you think was your best buy?

My best buy was Stan Lynn from the Villa, although he cost me £500 he was a great man. He also cost me a £250 signing-on fee.

CHAPTER EIGHT
— *In Europe* —

A s a player I have been on a number of overseas tours: Sweden, May 1946, we played four and won three. Switzerland, May 1948, we played five, winning four and drawing one. Germany, Holland and Denmark, May 1952, we played and won six, scoring 23 goals and conceding seven. Our best victories were 6–2 against Flensburg and 5–0 against Armenia Bielgold. Switzerland, 1959, it started with a 5–2 victory over Lucerne and ended with a 7–0 win over Schaffhausen. I also played against foreign opposition in the Festival of Britain 1950–51.

Festival of Britain matches 1950–51
7 May 1950 v Airdrie (h) 3–5
Scorers: Berry 2, Kelly (og)
12 May 1950 v Dinamo Yugoslavia (h) 0–2
18 May 1950 v Home Farm (Dublin) (a) 2–1
Scorers: Stewart, Berry
20 May 1950 v Cork Athletic (a) 5–2
Scorers: Trigg 2, Higgins, Stewart, Dailey

Even the first match under the floodlights at St Andrew's was against a German side, Borussia Dortmund, with whom we drew 3–3 on 31 October 1956 (See Chapter Eleven – Memorable Games).

I was lucky enough to be a pioneer with the Blues into formal European competition, such as the Inter-Cities Fairs Cup, which is now known as the UEFA Cup.

Inter-Cities Fairs Cup 1956–58

Group B

15 May 1956 v Internazionale Milan (a) 0–0

Attendance: 8,000

21 May 1956 v Zagreb Select (a) 1–0

Scorers: Brown

Attendance: 12,000

3 December 1956 v Zagreb Select (h) 3–0

Scorers: Orritt, Brown, Murphy

Attendance: 40,144

17 April 1957 v Internazionale Milan (h) 2–1

Scorers: Govan 2

Attendance: 34,461

Group B Final Table

	P	W	D	L	F	A	Pts
Birmingham City	4	3	1	0	6	1	7
Internazionale Milan	4	2	1	1	6	2	5
Zagreb Select	4	0	0	4	0	9	0

Semi-final first leg

23 October 1957 v Barcelona (h) 4–3

Merrick, Farmer, Allen, Larkin, Smith, Watts, Astall, Orritt, Brown, Neal, Murphy.

Scorers: Murphy 2, Brown, Orritt

Attendance: 30,791

Semi-final second leg

13 November 1957 v Barcelona (a) 0–1

Merrick, Hall, Allen, Larkin, Smith, Neal, Astall, Kinsey, Brown, Murphy, Govan.

Attendance: 60,000

Semi-final second leg replay

26 November 1957 v Barcelona (n*) 1–2

Merrick, Hall, Farmer, Watts, Smith, Neal, Astall, Orritt, Brown, Murphy, Govan.

Scorers: Murphy

Attendance: 20,000

* Played at St Jacob Stadium, Basel, Switzerland

It was great playing in Europe, every game we played we were pitting ourselves against the very best players in terms of skill and technique. But just like today's Premier League any mistake was punished. Nothing confirms that more than our experience in the semi-final replay of the 1958–60 tournament. We had beaten Barcelona at home 4–3 in October 1957 and then lost 1–0 over in Spain. Kubala, who scored their goal, was a fantastic player but he was yards offside for the 'equaliser'. The replay was played in Switzerland in November in icy conditions and we were 1–1 until Dick Neal, for some reason, decided to play the ball across his own box, which against normal opposition we might have got away with, but Kubala, being the player he was, nipped in and got the winner.

Inter-Cities Fairs Cup 1958–60

The competition was changed to a knockout system.

Round one first leg

14 October 1958 v Cologne Select (a) 2–2

Scorers: Neal, Hooper

Attendance: 12,000

Round one second leg

11 November 1958 v Cologne Select (h) 2–0

Scorers: Larkin, Taylor

Attendance: 20,266

Round two first leg

6 May 1959 v Dinamo Zagreb (h) 1–0

Scorer: Larkin

Attendance: 21,411

Round two second leg

24 May 1959 v Dinamo Zagreb (a) 3–3

Scorers: Larkin 2, Hooper

Attendance: 50,000

Semi-final first leg

7 October 1959 v Union St Gilloise (a) 4–2

Merrick, Sissons, Farmer, Watts, Smith, Neal, Hooper, Gordon, Orritt, Barrett, Taylor.

Scorers: Hooper, Gordon, Barrett, Taylor

Attendance: 20,000

Semi-final second leg

11 November 1959 v Union St Gilloise (h) 4–2 (aggregate 8–4)

Schofield, Farmer, Allen, Watts, Smith, Larkin, Hellawell, Barrett, Gordon, Hooper, Taylor.

Scorers: Gordon 2, Larkin, Hooper (pen)

Attendance: 14,152

Final first leg

29 March 1960 v Barcelona (h) 0–0

Schofield, Farmer, Allen, Watts, Smith, Neal, Astall, Gordon, Weston, Orritt, Hooper.

Attendance: 40,524

Final second leg

4 May 1960 v Barcelona (a) 1–4 (aggregate 1–4)

Schofield, Farmer, Allen, Watts, Smith, Neal, Astall, Gordon, Weston, Murphy, Hooper.

Blues scorer: Hooper (85)

Barcelona scorers: Martinez (3), Czibor (6, 49), Coll (78)

Attendance: 75,000

I played in the first two games of the competition and in the semi-final first leg before retiring for a second time. Everyone at the club was thrilled to have made a major European Final.

By the time of the second leg of the Final I had been appointed manager – what a baptism of fire!

Inter-Cities Fairs Cup 1960–61

Bertie Auld remembers: We were due to play Internazionale in the Inter-Cities Fairs Cup semi-final. It was my debut and I had only been with the players for literally a couple of hours. Gil's team talk was great, he said 'I've seen Bertie play and I like what he has to offer. I just want him to go out there and play, if he does that it will be great for Birmingham City Football Club.'

Round one first leg

19 October 1960 v Ujpesti Dozsa (h) 3–2

Scorers: Gordon 2, Astall

Attendance: 23,381

Round one second leg

26 October 1960 v Ujpesti Dozsa (a) 2–1

Scorers: Rudd, Singer

Attendance: 25,000

Round two first leg

23 November 1960 v Boldklub Copenhagen (a) 4–4

Scorers: Gordon 2, Singer 2

Attendance: 2,500

Round two second leg

7 December 1960 v Boldklub Copenhagen (h) 5–0

Scorers: Stubbs 2, Harris, Bloomfield, Hellawell

Attendance: 22,486

Semi-final first leg

19 April 1961 v Internazionale Milan (a) 2–1

Scorers: Harris, Balleri (og)

Attendance: 20,000

Semi-final second leg

3 May 1961 v Internazionale Milan (h) 2–1

Scorers: Harris 2

Attendance: 29,530

Final first leg

27 September 1961 v AS Roma (h) 2–2

Blues: Schofield, Farmer, Sissons, Hennessey, Foster, Beard, Hellawell, Bloomfield, Harris, Orritt, Auld.

Blues scorers: Hellawell (80), Orritt (87)

AS Roma scorers: Manfredini (30, 62)

Attendance: 21,050

Final second leg

11 October 1961 v AS Roma (a) 0–2 (aggregate 2–4)

Blues: Schofield, Farmer, Sissons, Hennessey, Smith, Beard, Hellawell, Bloomfield, Harris, Singer, Orritt.

Attendance: 50,000

Final first leg

21,050 fans filed into St Andrew's to see the first leg of the Inter-Cities Fairs Cup against Roma. Blues started on the attack early in the first half, with attempts from Bloomfield and Hennessey just a little off target. The Roma 'keeper, standing at over six feet, was a great presence in the goalmouth and it was his skill and agility which kept Blues scoring down to a bare minimum. Auld in the Blues attack was on particularly good form for this game. Hellawell put in a fine shot across the goal, but it posed no real threat and went out to safety. The Italian side had a tough job on their hands and found it hard to break through the Blues midfield, consisting of Beard, Foster and Hennessey. Blues stood strong, but their efforts could not hold Roma forever. Orlando was fouled but he evaded Sissons in defence to send the ball across goal to Manfredini, who put the ball into the back of the net in the 30th minute.

The second half started with Blues attacking with the same enthusiasm that they had in the first period. Second attempts were sent across the goalmouth before being swept away out of danger. The Italians seemed to have slowed down in attack, so it was a wake-up call for Blues when they managed to slip through to score a second goal. Menichelli made an attempt at goal, but it was cleared by Beard, only to bounce to Manfredini who again sent the ball over the line with ease.

Blues were determined not to give in easily and put up a gallant fight, giving Cudicini in the Roma goal a heavy workout. They spent a good 15 minutes raining attempts on the 'keeper, and some of the saves he pulled off were outstanding. The scoreline showed Blues the cold hard fact that they were two goals down with just 10 more minutes of play remaining. Hellawell then had a go at goal himself and this time Cudicini was well beaten by his shot. Blues took advantage and stepped up their attacks. Harris watched his shot bounce off the crossbar and rebound to Orritt who won back possession. He sent the ball goalwards from close range and it went over the line for the equaliser.

Final second leg

Gil remembers: Pestrin, who scored the second goal, was literally frothing at the mouth. Whether he was on some sort of drugs I do not know, but it was a hell of a match, which was made worse by the referee who was diabolical. Stanley Rous, who at the time was secretary of the FA, was sitting alongside me on the bench and was as unhappy with the refereeing as I was. He told me, 'I'll see this goes further'. The match deteriorated. Their coach had a go at me and I had a go at him – it was mayhem. There's that classic photograph of me in my suit going onto the pitch to try and bring order to the chaos. The real blow for me was at the evening banquet when Stanley Rous was asked to say a few words, and he included the following: 'I'd like to congratulate the referee on his performance.' Typical FA politics.

Inter-Cities Fairs Cup 1961–62

Round one

Birmingham City received a bye

Round two first leg

15 November 1961 v RCD Espanol (a) 2–5

Scorers: Bloomfield, Harris (pen)

Attendance: 60,000

Round two second leg

7 December 1961 v RCD Espanol (h) 1–0

Scorers: Auld

Attendance: 16,874

CHAPTER NINE
— Outside Football —

Although the club virtually owned the players in those days, I was handled very well by Birmingham City during my time as a player. While in the army I had been in the Physical Training Corps and through a contact of mine, Charlie Grove the Warwickshire County Cricket fast bowler, I heard about a job, as sports master at a school called Greenmore College, one of the top schools in the area. I had an interview with the principal, Mr Barney Morris, who asked me whether I was interested. I said I was and got the job, but it was subject to the approval of the club as it was a full-time role! The next day I spoke with Bob Brocklebank, putting forward the following proposal: Monday was a day off for footballers so there would be no conflict there. Tuesday morning was the main training session and I would attend that, but the rest of the week I would be excused training and would work for the school. Obviously I would be available for all games and indeed if extra games came along the school promised to modify the timetable on my behalf. Without hesitation he agreed on that basis. The school was happy with those arrangements and I went on to spend nine extremely happy years there, only leaving because I got the manager's job.

During those nine years the school enjoyed national success in cricket, athletics and swimming, but we lost at football! There was never any resentment from the players about my two jobs, although I always made sure that they knew my summer break was a paid holiday, which got Boydy (Len Boyd) spitting blood!

Did you enjoy playing cricket instead of football?

As a kid I was sports mad and quite the all-rounder. I carried off all the running prizes against local kids. Along with my sister Joan, who eventually ran for Birchfield Harriers, we regularly won all the prizes at the sports days organised for the road. We did so consistently well one year that the organisers barred us from taking part. This was the first controversy of my sporting life and after some debate we were allowed to participate. Perhaps rather tactlessly, we went on to win all the prizes again! So the chance to become a sports master was right up my street.

I ran the Blues' cricket team, of which regular members were Frank Mitchell, who played for Warwickshire, Ted Purdon, Gordon Astall and Graham Sissons, all decent players. I played a good standard and opened the batting for Walmley Cricket Club. We played a lot, mainly in benefit games for local cricketers. I remember we raised £300 for Charlie Groves, the Warwickshire fast bowler, one Sunday at the BSA ground. Charlie had a daughter at Greenmore College, hence the connection. We also did a benefit game for Tom Pritchard, another fast bowler.

 ## What jobs did you do outside of sport?

S & U was founded in Birmingham in 1938 and originally sold leisure and household goods – hence its name Sports and Utilities.

I worked for S & U as personnel manager for 35 years. I am qualified in personnel management, or human resources as they call it today, and I always had this desire to help people, and through the personnel function I was able to satisfy that need. During my playing career Bill Camkin, who was MD of Birmingham City and a cracking bloke, asked me what I did with my afternoons. Many of the lads spent their free time in the bookies, snooker rooms or pubs, but I was not interested in any of that. Bill said he had a pal who ran a gas cooker company in Leamington and he needed some help. I was there for between four to five months and would travel by train from Bordesley to Leamington every afternoon. I learnt so much about the business and I got paid my expenses!

I had applied for a job with S & U and while I was on cricket tour in Devon I was approached by CC (Clifford Coombs – The Blues and S & U owner). CC sponsored our cricket tour which alternated between London one year and Devon the next. I was always a keen cricketer and played for Warwickshire Seconds and Smethwick in the Birmingham League as a batsman and opening bowler. Anyway we were playing in Devon and CC had come down and was watching the game from his Rolls-Royce that was parked on the edge of the cricket ground. I was told that CC wanted to see me. When I went over he informed me that he knew I had applied for the (role of) personnel manager and asked me a few questions. I must have given the right answers because he asked me to come in and see his sons Keith and Derek. I got the job, which was good because I had only got a six month pay-off from the Blues. I was based at the head office in the Bull Ring, Birmingham. We had 20 branches and I was responsible for 200 people at its peak. While I was at S & U the Blues connection continued because we employed Cyril Trigg and Len Boyd as travellers. I retired from there at the age of 75.

 ## What has your family life been like?

I have been married twice, initially to Jean, who died 11 years ago after 50 years of marriage. We had two children, Neil who is now 57 and lives in Bournemouth, and Gill who is 59 and lives in Ireland. I have got five grandchildren and two great-grandchildren.

My first wedding was on 30 December 1944, in the morning, which meant I missed the afternoon game against Walsall in the League North Cup qualifying game. We won 3–1 thanks to a Trigg hat-trick and Sidney King deputised for me.

On 20 April 2007 I married my long-term partner Ivy, who was a fashion buyer at S & U and still works in fashion today.

 How long have you lived in Solihull?

My first house as an adult was in Braemar Road in Olton. We had Dave Massart and Wilson Jones as near neighbours. Wilson liked a drink after training and I would often see him staggering home in the late afternoon.

After that I occupied a club house at No. 56 Bray's Road, Sheldon, and then I moved to No. 28 Bills Lane in 1961.

 How is your health now?

I am something of a bionic man after three new hips (one went wrong), a triple heart bypass, prostate removal, surgery to the tendons in my fingers and a slight stroke 18 months ago.

It annoys me that I cannot get around as quickly as I used to be able to because of the stroke, but in myself I feel as well as I have ever done.

CHAPTER TEN
Personal Thoughts

Y ou have now reached the penultimate chapter of my book and I hope it has been as enjoyable to read as it has been for me to sit in my lounge recounting my memories to Keith. This is not my first book as I became a published author 35 years ago when *I See it All* was published in 1954. It was an unusual book because it was split into two parts: the first part was about my life up until then, while the second half was a guide to the art of goalkeeping.

Just like this it was ghostwritten, on this occasion by a local sports journalist, Charles Harrold. It did not make much money, mainly due to the fact that we had to pay Trevor Ford £250 when he won a court case for defamation. The legal furore caused something of a precedent with other autobiographies; one involved another international goalkeeper of my era, Jack Kelsey. Jack's ghostwriter, Brian Glanville, wrote in the *Sports Star Weekly* in 2006:

It was eight years later that I published another ghosted autobiography, *Over The Bar*, with the talented Wales and Arsenal goalkeeper Jack Kelsey. This time a fearful editor took out the most controversial and, in my view, intriguing elements in the book, running scared because a previous memoir by the England goalkeeper Gil Merrick had been successfully sued by Welsh International centre-forward Trevor Ford.

In Kelsey's case, it was the story of how Alec Stock was brought to Arsenal in the hope of imposing stricter discipline as assistant manager. Alec called a meeting and, to the horror of the players, told them 10 of them would be away at the end of the season.

He sent young winger Danny Clapton to tell Kelsey and left-back Denis

Evan to put out their cigarettes. They defiantly tapped their ash into the proffered ashtray and smoked on. It has long been a disappointment to me that this was excised. Stock didn't last long at Highbury.

Although my first book was not a huge financial success, it was very rewarding to see a book with my name on it on the shelves of the best booksellers in the country. *I See It All,* which is out of print now, cost nine shillings and sixpence – how times have changed.

Biographies and autobiographies are written by today's football stars before their careers have even started, let alone finished. I suppose it is another new way to make money. I do not envy their fat weekly pay cheques or their celebrity status because in my own career I benefitted in the same way, even though it was at a much more modest level. While I could never have reached the financial rewards enjoyed by today's footballers, I enjoyed a lifestyle that was significantly better than the average working man. I always had money in my pocket, a nice house, a smart car, good quality clothes and a lot of affection from the people in the street.

At that time you were virtually owned by the clubs, there were no agents and sponsorship deals were frowned upon. However, Quaker Oats were aware that to use a famous footballer as an endorsement of their product could increase their sales. After I had been capped by England they used an image of me on their box and I became involved in a promotion in the Lewis's department store in Birmingham. I had to stand in goal and face shots from customers. I cannot remember if I got paid, but it was not approved of by the club and I had to stop. One thing to remember though is that I still eat Quaker Oats for breakfast so it was never about the money!

While it is tremendous to be recognised by the man in the street, it is equally a thrill to be acknowledged by your peers. Charles Buchan published a monthly magazine entitled *Charles Buchan's Football Monthly* which was the definitive football magazine of its time. At the end of the 1951–52 season he selected me for his best XI of the season, which included:

Gil Merrick (Birmingham City), Johnny Carey (Manchester United), Lionel Smith (Arsenal), Billy Wright (Wolves), Harry Clarke (Spurs), Jimmy Dickinson (Portsmouth), Tom Finney (Preston North End), Johnny Morris (Derby), Derek Dooley (Sheffield Wednesday), Ivor Allchurch (Swansea), Bobby Mitchell (Newcastle).

Manager: Billy Walker (Nottingham Forest).

With little or no televised football in my day, appearances in magazines and books were the only way to raise your profile. It was a great honour to appear on the dust cover of the first edition of the *Charles Buchan's Soccer Gift Book.*

While there were obvious ways to be recognised as being good at your job, I was surprised and flattered that people saw fit to involve me in projects that had nothing to do with the day job. I did not know that Kevin Raymond, the football poet, was including me in his work entitled *Sweet Street Memories.*

> *Empty streets were Villa Park,*
> *Highbury, or The Den.*
> *When we first got this football lark*
> *Beside the River Thames.*

> *Games were all we lived for*
> *Anywhere we'd play*
> *Till our mams would shout 'Oi You! Indoors,*
> *Now! Or I'll lock that ball away'.*

Personal Thoughts

When the old man left the boozer
And staggered down our street
As a bellowing Evening Newsboy
Told us, if Chelsea had got beat.

We'd worship Frankie Blunstone,
Tambling and The Cat
Barry Bridges and Bert Murray
It was lovely, thinking back.

We'd heard about Bert Trautmann
Gil Merrick, Frankie Swift
The old man spoke of Duncan Edwards
'That young boy, sure had the gift'.

Watching Bobby Robson
Tosh Chamberlaine, Johnny Haynes
From that mob at Craven Cottage
I've an awful memory for names!

Frantic games in football cages
When the streets were out of bounds
In Cup replays that took ages
It would seem we played for hours.

Five a sides with tennis balls
Half inched from the toffs
Crab football played in dining halls
Where school lunches were scoffed.

Frightening cinders pitches
With stones and broken glass
Thinking that the rich kids
Were so blessed to play on grass.

Clapham Common, Battersea Park
Our Wembley, or The Bridge
In finals where we were the stars
As street football playing kids!

It was probably less of a surprise to me to be included in the Harvey Andrews song *Famous Men* because Harvey is a Bluenose through and through.

Let us now praise famous men
Cast their memories back when
They proudly wore the City's blue
And did their best for me and you.
No piles of gold, no Mercs, no 'posh'
They never got great wads of dosh.
They caught the bus, they lived next door
They played our game, they asked no more
In '56 they brought much joy
To me when I was just a boy.
The best Blues team there's ever been
Gil Merrick, and Jeff Hall, Ken Green,
Warhurst, Smith and Boyd closed down
The best there were and Eddie Brown
And Murphy helped by Kinsey too,

Took Astall's cross and put us through.
Then Gil retired but soon returned
To manage Blues, used all he'd learned
To build a side and made its mark
That won OUR Cup at Villa Park.
They pioneered in Europe too,
They beat the best, our boys in Blue.
Inter came and Inter fell,
They beat Barca once as well.
Zagreb, Ujpesti Dosza, Roma
St. Gilloise, another homer.
Now maybe the present team
Could, one day, fulfil the dream.
So we meet with memories clear
Of when we used to shout and cheer.
Spion Kop or Tilton Road, the Railway End
When train smoke blowed,
Those winter nights of freezing fog,
The floodlit pitch a shining bog.
Our jumps for joy, our tears of pain
No matter what, we came again.
So thanks to them and here's to you
Who wore our shirts of Royal Blue.
We'll not forget those great days
When you were, you are, our famous men.

Another thing that comes with recognition is nicknames. These are bestowed upon you without any approval! I was given three nicknames during my career. 'Mister Thirteen' is the most famous and was bestowed upon me after England conceded 13 goals in two games against the Mighty Magyars. Although I conceded those goals, statistically speaking I am not the worst England goalkeeper in history. That dubious honour goes to Upton Park's Conrad Warner, who conceded seven on his debut against Scotland in 1878 and unsurprisingly did not play again. For goalkeepers playing more than once, Pilgrims' Harry Swepstone let in 18 goals in six games during the 1880s.

The little-remembered nickname 'The Clutch' is another which I think came from my desire to always catch the ball. Goalkeeping has changed so much since I played. I just cannot understand how goalkeepers cause so much trouble by parrying the ball instead of catching it. I watch football on TV, look at the goals scored and see how many of them are scored from parries, they simply do not hold onto the ball. If a 'keeper cannot catch it then he should punch it. I do not see how goalkeepers can punch it clean with the big gloves they wear. I wore gloves when it was wet but today they wear gloves in all weather. They look like frying pans don't they?

My favourite nickname was 'Eccles'. When I was stationed at Oswestry I was always hungry and would often devour 10 Eccles cakes at a time, so my squadron nickname became 'Eccles'. One Saturday, when we were playing at Stamford Bridge and I was warming up, I heard this voice shouting 'Eccles, Eccles'. After a while I realised the call was for me and recognised my corporal pal. I met him at the entrance after the game and we went for a drink and a chat.

In my career I only had one real superstition and that was to always go onto the pitch after the skipper. For me, the goalkeeper is Number One, there has never been a truly successful side without a top-class 'keeper. Having said that, the captain is the most important member of any team, and therefore, in my mind, it made sense for the 'keeper to follow the captain onto the field. I did it for England behind the great Billy Wright and also for the best Blues captain I played for, Len Boyd.

A funny thing about Len was that he was terrified of flying. The old Hamburg stadium had been rebuilt following the war and the opening match was in 1950. A team of 12 players from Blues, Villa, Albion and Wolves had been chosen, including Peter Murphy, George Edwards, Len and myself. We got to the airport and Len refused to go, he was that frightened.

The great thing about writing a book so late in life is that I can now set the record straight on a number of things; for instance, it has always been assumed that I modelled my play on that of Harry Hibbs – this is totally wrong. It was in the middle of 1946 that I was made aware of a newspaper article that said, 'I regard Merrick as the most stylish goalkeeper since Harry Hibbs. In fact he has moulded his style on this master goalkeeper.' I only saw Hibbs play twice, and the first time I took any real notice of him was when I went to watch the Blues play Liverpool with Shirley Juniors. We had won a Cup Final in the morning and the visit to the match was a reward. I stood behind the goal but I cannot remember anything about Hibbs's performance that day. The second time was an end of season game against Everton, and I was more impressed with their goalkeeper, Ted Sagar. In fact, Sagar was my schoolboy hero and I could not take my eyes off him that day, he was so confident in his play, which I realised must have made it difficult for forwards, and I decided there and then to model myself on Ted, not Harry. It was the same in cricket, my hero was Wally Hammond and I tried to bat just like him.

It never fails to surprise me that people are still interested in my career. I often get telephone calls from fans from all corners of the country asking whether they can visit me to get something signed, take a photograph or simply have a chat. I really enjoy their visits and it gets me thinking about subjects I had long since forgotten, it is so wonderful that people remember me. Some of the things they recall I had completely forgotten. The following anecdotes illustrate this:

One of my army mates recalled the time we went into a pub in Chester which was run by Dixie Dean, the greatest centre-forward of all time. Some of the lads told him that I was in the pub and he came over for a chat and knew who I was – I was thrilled!

Ron Wylie, then of Notts County, scored four goals against me on 19 April 1952 away in a 5–0 defeat in front of 24,360 people. Ron went on to play for Birmingham and the Villa in the 1960s.

On 5 April 1952 I saved a penalty from Bill Eckersley of Blackburn Rovers (my England teammate) but Bill recovered to head home the rebound, a rare headed penalty. Blues won the game 4–1.

As I said in the preface of this book, I am often asked what was my best Blues side, and I am also asked what was my best England side and who were the best players I played against, so here goes:

My best England side made up of players I played with would be (including myself):

Bill Eckersley

Alf Ramsey

Billy Wright

Harry Johnston

Jimmy Dickinson

Tom Finney

Len Shackleton

Nat Lofthouse

Jim Hagan

Stan Matthews

The best players I played against were:

Bert Williams (Wolves)

Ted Ditchburn (Spurs)

Bert Trautmann (Manchester City)

John Charles (Leeds)

Ernst Ocwirk (Austria)

Ladislao Kubala (Barcelona)

Ferenc Puskas (Hungary)

Jackie Milburn (Newcastle)

Ray Barlow (West Bromwich Albion)

Ronnie Allen (West Bromwich Albion)

I realise how lucky I have been and there have been very few disappointments over the years. However, apart from my sacking there have been two other major upsets in my career; our defeat in the 1956 FA Cup Final and the death of Jeff Hall.

An FA Cup runners'-up medal is totally worthless. The feeling of utter despair you cannot describe, completely at odds to winning the semi-final at Hillsborough, that was a fantastic feeling of elation. I remember Jeff Hall doing a handstand in front of me, he was so happy. I remember being with Harry Johnston of Blackpool when they won the Cup in 1953 after losing in 1952 and he said, 'There's only one way to be at Wembley and that's as a winner,' and he was absolutely right.

Jeff Hall's death was an immense shock to everyone connected with the Blues. We had played at Portsmouth on Saturday 21 March 1959 and drew 1–1, Bunny Larkin scoring in front of a crowd of 18,149. The team was made up of myself, Hall, Allen, Watts, Smith, Hume, Astall, Gordon, Stubbs, Larkin and Hooper. Everyone had got in the communal bath (as it was in those days), but Jeff Hall did not travel back with the lads, he had got a lift home because he was due to referee a youth game that was being run in Birmingham on behalf of a Sunday newspaper. The rest of us stayed overnight in Portsmouth. The following Monday I was getting ready to go to (Greenmore) college when Ken Fish appeared at my door saying, 'Gil, you can't go out until further notice because Jeff is under observation with an undiagnosed condition'. All training was suspended and within two to three days Jeff was diagnosed as having polio. We did not train for two weeks as Jeff deteriorated and finally died a few weeks later. It was a terrible time for everyone at the club as they suspected that he had contracted the disease in the communal bath at Portsmouth, so we were all very lucky when we eventually got the all-clear.

With Gil's permission, I have contacted a number of his ex-colleagues to give them the opportunity to contribute to this book, and here are a few of their insights into 'Mr Birmingham City'.

Alex Govan

Gil Merrick is Birmingham City, when you talk about the Blues you are talking about Gil Merrick, he's Birmingham through and through!

He was a great 'keeper and a nice chap. He owned the Blues Café that was near to St Andrew's in Cattell Road.

Of course, we did not see much of Gil during the week, he came in on Tuesday when we normally had a practice match and then on Friday for the pre-match meeting. Gil could get away with that being a 'keeper. I think it would have been more difficult for an outfield player. But it was never a problem. It did not affect his performances because if it had Johnny Schofield, who was a good 'keeper, would have played more games. Of course, Gil was football mad so if it had been a problem he would have given up the school job.

He was not a mouthy type, he was easy to get on with. Most 'keepers had funny ways or were a bit temperamental and if a goal went in it was always someone else's fault – but not Gil.

After my playing days were over I ran the Hyde Park pub in Plymouth, which was a 10-minute walk across a park from Argyle's ground. After a game a few of the Blues players came into the pub and stayed for afters in my private quarters. Early in the morning the doorbell rang and it was Gil asking if any of his players were there as he had done a count at the Grand Hotel on Plymouth Hoe and found a few were missing.

Bertie Auld

The first thing you notice about Gil is his presence, both physically and in terms of personality.

I was at Celtic and had been dropped to the reserves. We were playing Hearts at Tynecastle on a Wednesday night. After the game I was in the dressing room when in came Gil Merrick. He looked directly at me and said, 'I want to sign you'. He was extremely well-dressed and he took my breath away with his directness, and his eyes were so bright, shiny and honest.

At the time I was single and living at home with my parents. Dad had a passion for football but my mom just wanted the best for her son. My career was at a crossroads, I had an offer from John Carey, manager of Everton, to join Bobby Collins there, but I was told by my dad to listen to any offers carefully. I did not see eye to eye with the chairman at Celtic, Robert Kelly, so I did need a move and he told me there was an interested club. I asked him who it was but he would not tell me.

Later I was training in the stadium, just me and the manager Jim McGorry, when I was told that an English club had made an offer which

Celtic had accepted and would I like to speak to them. Of course, it was then I realised who Gil Merrick was, he had sold himself to me and the club so I did not hesitate to travel down to Blues for further talks.

I travelled down by train and was met at The Midlands Hotel by Gil and Don Dorman (chief scout), who was also very positive about the club. The next day I met the board and the deal was done.

St Andrew's reminded me of Celtic Park and I felt that Blues was a family club, but Gil was a big plus, he wanted me to play for him.

While I was there we had some great players but the team never fulfilled its potential.

Not long after joining the Blues I got married and Gil organised us a two-bedroom apartment on Richmond Road, Solihull, in which we lived happily during my time at the Blues. I recall one night I was ill and we had no telephone but we got a message to Gil and at one o'clock in the morning he turned up with a doctor. Great Man.

Jack Lane

Gil is nine years older than me so I used to watch him play when I was at school, and what a 'keeper he was, never showy, very calm and he always got his angles nigh on perfect.

When I signed for the Blues in September 1949 I was amazed that he would even speak to us let alone be helpful – he knew how to speak to youngsters through his work at Greenmore.

He was a great bloke to be with, there was never any side on him. Mind you in those days it would have been knocked out of him by the likes of Len Boyd, Ken Green, Cyril Trigg, etc.

He was best man at my wedding and we had a good party that night and on other occasions. I remember one at Sunderland with Ted Purdon who used to play for Blues.

Colin Withers

As a young professional I was helped tremendously by Gil and John Schofield. There were no bad feelings between any of us. I felt privileged to have two great 'keepers teaching me the tricks of the trade. When Gil retired it was inevitable that Schoey would take over and to my mind he was as good as Gil on his day.

John Vincent

Gil was a tremendous bloke, very fair, and once, after I had finished playing, we met and he told me I should have played for England. That was nice. You had your own feelings on his sacking but you just had to get on with it. But I know it took Gil a long time to go back to Birmingham. When you have given your life to a club and all of a sudden you are out, you can understand his position.

Terry Hennessey

I had been at the club about 12 months when Gil called me in and said they were going to release me. I cried my eyes out and begged for another chance. Gil told me in later life that it was a wake-up call. I will never know if they were serious about getting rid of me, but Gil was a strong man and if it had been in his mind I would have gone. But he gave me another chance and I did not need telling twice. Gil is as honest as the day is long and someone for whom all the players had the greatest respect.

John Schofield

Without doubt the best goalkeeper in the air I ever watched was Gil Merrick. You never saw Gil making fantastic spectacular saves because he used his positional sense and wonderful hands to erase the danger before it matured.

This book must end where it started, with my departure from the place where I had devoted my professional career. From reading this book you will have realised the impact David 'Tapper' Wiseman had on me.

David Wiseman was born in 1885, which coincidentally was the year BCFC adopted professionalism. As an eight-year-old he used to gain free admission to Muntz Street by carrying the players' kits into the dressing room. He was appointed to the board in 1928. His voice became well-known to radio listeners when he made the FA Cup draw as chairman of the Challenge Cup Committee. In the mid-1950s David, in his late 70s, had to undergo major life-saving surgery. The operation was a success, but he was warned that he was living on borrowed time. He kept going for another 20 years, during which time he was vice-chairman and president of the club. He died in 1978 at the age of 93. His son Jack now acts as vice-chairman.

One episode that sums up the man for me took place while the Birmingham City youth team were on tour in Switzerland. They had won a pre-match game before the full international between England and Switzerland in which I was playing. Our youth team had kicked them off the park and were literally booed off the pitch.

Later that night at the England hotel I got a call to go to David Wiseman's room (he had got the flu) and was amazed that all he wanted to say to me was, 'What will they think of me after that performance from our youth team?' They, of course, were the International Committee who knew he was a BCFC director. I thought that was typical of the man, always thinking of his reputation.

I did not go back to St Andrew's until 2006, 42 years after my sacking, and only then because it was Malcolm's (Page) testimonial and he wanted me to present his plaque at half-time. I left immediately afterwards.

Ten years after my sacking I mellowed, old players do, but for so long I lost interest in the game and in the Blues. I went back into football management with Bromsgrove Rovers and Atherstone United, but unfortunately it was the same scenario again – after three seasons the committees began to interfere and I left!

There is little doubt that loyalty is an admirable quality but one which holds little value in the world of professional football. It is as true today as it was in the 1950s and 1960s. If playing today, I would be driving a Bentley, living in a mansion and playing for a club that has nothing to do with my birthplace or upbringing.

CHAPTER ELEVEN
— *Memorable Games* —

During my conversations with Gil we have identified 10 games he considers to be memorable outside of those featured in other chapters.

1. v Derby County, FA Cup semi-final, 23 March 1946   **Drew 1–1**

Played at Hillsborough, Sheffield.

Blues: Merrick, Duckhouse, Jennings, Harris, Turner, Mitchell, Mulraney, Dougall, Jones, Bodle, Edwards.
Scorer: Mulraney
Attendance: 65,015

2. v Derby County, FA Cup semi-final replay, 27 March 1946   **Lost 0–4**

Played at Maine Road, Manchester.

Blues: Merrick, Duckhouse, Jennings, Harris, Turner, Mitchell, Mulraney, Dougall, Jones, Bodle, Edwards.
Attendance: 80,407
Gate Receipts: £28,205

In the FA Cup semi-final in 1946 when we drew 1–1 with Derby County, I remember that Raich Carter handled the ball before they scored. Had the referee seen it and penalised him, who knows what the final result might have been. Before the match Harry Storer had told us that their goalkeeper, Vic Woodley, was weak on his right-hand side, and when Bodle had the chance to win the game in the last minute, he shot tamely to the right and Woodley saved it!

In the 1946 semi-final replay we lost it in the second half. It was 0–0 at half-time and the moment that turned the game was when Peter Doherty, on his way to scoring, went in late on Ted Duckhouse and broke his leg. We were forced to play with 10 men and we eventually lost 4–0.

We were drawing with only half a minute to go to the end of ordinary time when Harry Bodle, our inside-forward, was sent clear about 20 yards from the Derby goal. Woodley, who had been bought from Bath City as a stopgap, was the Derby goalkeeper, and to everyone's amazement he stayed on his line. It was surely a gift. Bodle took the ball within eight yards of the goal but hit it so near to Woodley that the 'keeper was able to beat the ball away. We were beaten in extra-time and Derby went on to win the Cup. In the dressing room after the Maine Road replay Arthur Turner just sat with his head in his hands, almost on the verge of a breakdown. In the last season of a fine career he had been so near and yet so far from Wembley in one second of play.

3. v Sheffield Wednesday (a) 24 April 1948   Drew 0–0

Penultimate game of the season.

Blues: Merrick, Green, Jennings, Harris, Duckhouse, Mitchell, Stewart, Dougall, Trigg, Bodle, Edwards.
Attendance: 25,990

Blues won their 59th point of the season to reach their best-ever total under the two points for a win rule. They lost only three away games all season and were undefeated in 37 of 42 games. They conceded only 24 goals, equalling the 1900–01 season (13 at home and 11 away). Played 42, Won 22, Drawn 15, Lost 5, Goals For 65, Goals Against 24, Points 59.

There were some great characters in the promotion team of 1948: Arthur 'Tosher' Turner, 'Big Frank' Mitchell, Neil 'Tadge' Dougall and George

Edwards who was an intellectual and kept a diary of every game. I kept 22 clean sheets in 36 appearances, which I believe is still a record 40 years on.

It was the end of the 1947–48 season; in fact, the last match but one of the season. We had to get a point against Sheffield Wednesday at Hillsborough to win the Second Division Championship – and we did it. There were unforgettable scenes in our dressing room after the game. Everyone wanted to shout and sing and congratulate everyone else at the same time. There was an atmosphere in the room that day that I have never experienced since. It was a moment of the greatest joy that only a team game like football can bring. And what a team we had been, for not only had we taken the championship but we had set up a new 'low goals against' record for the Football League – 24 goals in 42 matches! It is often said in football that it is impossible to plan success. It may be that Birmingham City in the 1947–48 season was the exception that proves the rule because our winning of the championship was a planned defensive triumph. From the very start our manager, Mr Harry Storer, worked to a blackboard plan, and it was a plan, or a method of play if you like, that never once varied. Theoretically it couldn't go wrong, and so expert were our players in carrying out the man-for-man marking and deep covering scheme, that it failed on only 24 occasions in 42 matches of 90 minutes each.

4. v Blackpool, FA Cup semi-final, 10 March 1951   Drew 0–0

Played at Maine Road, Manchester.

Blues: Merrick, Green, Badham, Boyd, Atkins, Ferris, Stewart, Higgins, Trigg, Smith, Berry.
Attendance: 70,000

Jackie Stewart hit the post with the last kick of the game.

5. v Blackpool, FA Cup semi-final replay, 14 March 1951   **Drew 1–2**

Played at Goodison Park.

Blues: Merrick, Green, Badham, Boyd, Atkins, Ferris, Stewart, Higgins, Trigg, Smith, Berry.

Blues scorer: Smith (64)

Blackpool scorers: Mortenson (4), Perry (63)

Attendance: 70,114

Gate receipts: £15,000

When we played Blackpool in March 1951 in the semi-final and Jackie Stewart hit the post with virtually the last kick of the game, guess who dribbled the ball away from the goal? Stanley Matthews. Stan did not like playing against Jack Badham because Jack was as quick as Stan over 10 to 15 yards.

Every goalkeeper knows despair in some degree when he is beaten. He may do the right thing, in the sense that he takes up the correct position, but something goes wrong elsewhere. But it is when a goal is scored as a direct result of one's own mistake that despair hangs heavily. And when it happens in a vitally important match and leaves one feeling that it has turned the game, then that despair knows no bounds. It was that way with me in the FA Cup semi-final against Blackpool in 1951. We had drawn the first match at Maine Road and replayed at Goodison Park. Early in the replay Stan Mortensen got the ball clear on the edge of the 18-yard line. With a defender closing in, he had to shoot there and then. It was a real Mortensen crack, going across me and heading for the far top corner. I reached for it with both hands but got only one to the ball. The result was that the force of the ball turned my hand inwards and the ball was diverted into the net. It wasn't the winning goal, or the only goal – the result was 2–1 – but it meant that for nearly all the game we were fighting against a deficit and in a semi-final that is hardly a happy position in which to be. In moments like that a goalkeeper is tested to the full. His mistakes can bring despair to his team, but no one feels it more than himself. Nevertheless, he has got to throw it off more quickly perhaps than the rest, and to do that he must have the right temperament. And herein lies the moral.'

6. v Doncaster Rovers (a) 4 May 1955   Won 5–1

Last game of the season, Birmingham were promoted as champions of Division Two.

Blues: Schofield, Hall, Badham, Boyd, Smith, Warhurst, Astall, Kinsey, Brown, Murphy, Govan.
Blues scorers: Astall (38, 73), Murphy (55), Brown (65), Govan (90)
Doncaster Rovers scorers: J. Walker (44)
Attendance: 21,303
Merrick: 27 Appearances, 0 Goals.

Blues finally did it! Promotion at last to the First Division, where they had not been since they were relegated in 1950. In a double bonus they also secured the Second Division Championship, pipping Luton. A crowd of 21,303 watched the match, including many travelling Blues fans, and also followers of Rotherham who would have benefitted from a slip-up by Blues. Blues had to win this game, and they did so with an emphatic four-goal burst in a one-sided second half which eventually ended with a 5–1 scoreline.

The opening minutes were a typical tense clash of biting tackles and goalmouth excitement, Blues taking advantage of a strong wind by loading high crosses which Hardwick often had difficulty with. However, he kept them out with an array of improvised goalkeeping manoeuvres. The importance of the first goal was such that Blues allowed gaps in their defence to appear. Doncaster took advantage of these and Schofield did well to keep out a Jimmy Walker attempt. Moments later the 'keeper again pulled out a spectacular save from Geoff Walker which had been deflected on its way towards him. After 38 minutes, however, the pressure from Blues paid off when Astall scored. Latching onto a pass from Murphy, he outclassed the Rovers defence and, although his shot was blocked by Hardwick, followed up to hammer in the rebound. This brought about more pressure from Blues as they pushed for another to wrap up the game. However, despite forcing three quick corners, it was Doncaster on a breakaway who got the game's second goal just a minute before half-time. Jimmy Walker rose to plant his header past Schofield from only the second corner of the game. So typically Blues, after dominating the first half they were now level at the break and needing another goal. Again they would have to do it the difficult way.

The second half started much in the manner as the first, only this time Blues put their chances away. The first came after 55 minutes, Hardwick again only half saving a shot by Murphy who picked up the rebound to score via the inside of the post. Just 10 minutes later Brown controlled a cross from Hall skilfully enough to turn and fire past Hardwick. There was no restraining Blues now, and after 73 minutes Brown went through on a weaving run which opened up Rovers' defence again. He then waited at the edge of the area and lobbed a pass to Astall to volley in Blues' fourth. A memorable night ended perfectly when, right on the final whistle, Govan scored a fifth goal and the championship celebrations started in earnest.

It was the end of the 1954–55 season and we had to go to Doncaster knowing a win would clinch promotion to the First Division. I had been out for three weeks when Ray Shaw asked me, 'What about tomorrow? It's a big game.' John Schofield had deputised for me and had done well so I told Ray that I didn't think it would be right to drop him for the last game. Ray really wanted me to play but being the guy he was he respected my opinion and Schoey played.

At the time there was a rumour that one of the teams in contention for promotion had a collection of £5 per man to incentivise the opposition to go easy. When they approached the captain of the team they were told that they were too late as another team had already paid them to get stuck in! The pressure for promotion even in those days was immense.

7. v Sunderland, FA Cup semi-final, 17 March 1956   Won 3–0
Played at Hillsborough, Sheffield.

Blues: Merrick, Hall, Green, Boyd, Smith, Badham, Astall, Kinsey, Brown, Murphy, Govan.
Scorers: Kinsey, Astall, Brown
Attendance: 65,107

It was the FA Cup semi-final in 1956 against Sunderland at Hillsborough, Sheffield. The spirit in the club and the way we played were fantastic, we were so confident. Len Boyd was, in my opinion, a great captain and was responsible for the way the team was, both on and off the pitch. On the day it was even-steven, although we were 1–0 up thanks to a Noel Kinsey goal. As we were coming out for the second half Ted Purdon, who had played for the Blues and was a pal of mine and a good cricketer, spoke to me as we walked down the tunnel: 'Gil, watch your step, the manager's offered us an incentive of 200 Final tickets if we win.' It certainly worked as we were penned in for the next 20 minutes with Len Shackleton playing magnificent football. Eventually we scored a second and finally won the game 3–0. Even so, it was still tense and then a throw-in was given and I noticed the linesman put three fingers across his chest to indicate to the referee that there were three minutes left. They were a long three minutes, but we were there – Wembley in May.

8. v Portsmouth, FA Cup fourth round, (h) 25 January 1947 Won 1–0

The penalty save of my life.

Blues: Merrick, Duckhouse, Jennings, Harris, Turner, Dearson, Mulraney, Dougall, Trigg, Bodle, Edwards.
Scorer: Harris
Attendance: 30,000

This was the first full season after World War Two and I played every game bar one, on 17 May 1947. It was a fourth-round tie at home and we were leading through a rare Fred Harris goal when Pompey were awarded a penalty. They had a formidable penalty taker in Duggie Reid who had the nickname of 'Cannon-Ball'. His technique was to blast the ball as hard as he could but always on target. I dived to my left and managed to turn it round the post – the penalty save of my life!

9. v Liverpool (h) 11 December 1954 Won 9–1

Blues: Merrick, Hall, Green, Boyd, Smith, Warhurst, Astall, Lane, Brown, Larkin, Govan.

Scorers: 1–0 Lane (48 sec), 2–0 Brown (11), 3–0 Brown (16), 3–1 Liddell (19), 4–1 Astall (27), 5–1 Astall (49), 6–1 Murphy (54), 7–1 Govan (77), 8–1 Murphy (84), 9–1 Brown (85)

Attendance: 17,514

Always a great game for a goalkeeper when your forwards are your best form of defence. However, I did concede one. We were three up when Trevor Smith went AWOL and Billy Liddell raced onto a through ball from Payne and almost singed my moustache with a powerful drive from 15 yards out.

10. v Barcelona, Inter-Cities Fairs Cup, (a) 13 November 1957   Lost 0–1

Second leg match.

Blues: Merrick, Hall, Allen, Larkin, Smith, Neal, Astall, Kinsey, Brown, Murphy, Govan.

Attendance: 60,000

Bunny Larkin was involved in a rumpus, which was Bernard's way, but on this occasion it wasn't his fault. He was having a particularly good match against 'Laddie' Kubala when he got hurt. We had understood that substitutes could be fielded in the event of injuries. However, when our trainer tried to send Johnny Watts out in his place, the Barcelona players and officials refused to let him take over, and to make matters worse they were supported by the referee. I remember Bunny lying on the floor injured while all this commotion was going on. Eventually he had to carry on and we were virtually down to 10 men. Kubala suddenly had a lot more freedom, and it was no surprise when from what looked like an offside position he lobbed the ball over my head for the only goal.

Career Statistics

Club

Season	League	FA Cup	Europe	Total	Manager	Position
1945–46	0	8	0	8	Storer	
1946–47	41	4	0	45	Storer	third Division Two
1947–48	36	0	0	36	Storer	first Division Two
1948–49	41	2	0	43	Storer/Brocklebank	17th Division One
					January 1949	
1949–50	42	1	0	43	Brocklebank	22nd Division One
1950–51	42	6	0	48	Brocklebank	fourth Division Two
1951–52	41	2	0	43	Brocklebank	third Division Two
1952–53	35	7	0	42	Brocklebank	sixth Division Two
1953–54	38	2	0	40	Brocklebank	seventh Division Two
1954–55	27	4	0	31	Brocklebank/Turner	first Division Two
					November 1954	
1955–56	38	6	2	46	Turner	sixth Division One
1956–57	40	7	2	49	Turner	12th Division One
1957–58	28	1	3	32	Turner/Beasley	13th Division One
					February 1958	
1958–59	34	6	2	42	Turner/Beasley from	ninth Division One
					September 1958 Beasley	
1959–60	2	0	1	3	Beasley	19th Division One
Total	**485**	**56**	**10**	**551**		

In 551 games Gil conceded 666 goals, or 1.21 per game.

Representative

Football League XI, between 1947–54 he made 11 appearances: five against the Irish League, three against the League of Ireland and three against the Scottish League.

Season	Match	Season	Match
1945–46	APTC XI v FA XI	1951–52	Irish League
1947–48	Irish League	1952–53	Irish League
1948–49	League of Ireland	1952–53	Scottish League
1949–50	League of Ireland	1953–54	Irish League
1949–50	Irish League	1953–54	League of Ireland
1951–52	Scottish League	1953–54	Scottish League

Wartime

For the British army in 1946–47, Gil made three appearances: against the French in Paris, the Belgians in Brussels and BAOR in Germany.

Club

Season	Appearances	Season	Appearances
1939–40	1	1943–44	38
1940–41	13	1944–45	38
1941–42	8 Friendlies	1945–46	39
1942–43	35	TOTAL:	172

International

Type	Caps	Minutes	Type	Caps	Minutes
Friendly	13	1,170	HC	4	360
WC Qualifier	3	270	Competitive	10	930
WC Finals	3	300	**TOTAL:**	**23**	**2,100**

In 23 games Gil conceded 45 goals or 1.96 per game and he kept five clean sheets.

Club Records

Longest serving player

Gil Merrick   22 years   1938–60

Most club appearances (including wartime matches)

Gil Merrick   723   1940–59

Most senior appearances

Gil Merrick   551   1946–59

Consecutive appearances

Gil Merrick   145   1949–52

Consecutive League appearances

Gil Merrick   136   1949–52

Most clean sheets in a League season

Ian Bennett   21 (45 appearances)   1997–98 Division One

Gil Merrick   20 (36 appearances)   1947–48 Division Two

Manager

In 168 games his team scored 244 goals and conceded 347, amassing 134 points. He had a 39.9 per cent success rate and his team scored an average of 1.45 goals and conceded 2.07 per game.

Blues v Villa

Gil was involved in 20 Villa derbies as either player or manager. He won seven, drew seven and lost six.

Season	League	Date	Result	Score	Crowd	Venue	Status
1948–49	Division One	4 December	Won	3–0	61,632	Away	Player
1948–49	Division One	30 April	Lost	0–1	45,000	Home	Player
1949–50	Division One	10 December	Drew	1–1	44,520	Away	Player
1949–50	Division One	29 April	Drew	2–2	26,144	Home	Player
1955–56	Division One	5 September	Drew	0–0	57,690	Away	Player
1955–56	Division One	21 September	Drew	2–2	32,642	Home	Player
1956–57	Division One	27 October	Lost	1–3	35,595	Away	Player
1956–57	Division One	10 April	Lost	1–2	29,893	Home	Player
1957–58	Division One	24 August	Won	3–1	50,807	Home	DNP
1957–58	Division One	21 December	Won	2–0	39,889	Away	Player
1958–59	Division One	23 August	Drew	1–1	53,028	Away	Player
1958–59	Division One	20 December	Won	4–1	31,827	Home	Player
1960–61	Division One	22 October	Lost	2–6	46,306	Away	Manager
1960–61	Division One	11 March	Drew	1–1	41,645	Home	Manager
1961–62	Division One	28 October	Won	3–1	39,790	Away	Manager
1961–62	Division One	17 March	Lost	0–2	45,885	Home	Manager
1962–63	Division One	27 October	Won	3–2	42,207	Home	Manager
1962–63	Division One	16 March	Lost	0–4	46,680	Away	Manager
1963–64	Division One	30 March	Won	3–0	25,890	Away	Manager
1963–64	Division One	31 March	Drew	3–3	28,048	Home	Manager